OUR MIXTAPES, OURSELVES.

THE HAPPY-SAD STORY AND SOUNDTRACK OF GENERATION X.

DAVID GRADY

Marianne Monica Fiorillo
"Marianne"
Brown eyes, brown hair,
bashful, friend to all ... FU-
TURE PLANS...To be a tele-
phone operator ... HEART'S
DESIRE ... To become a wo-
man disc jockey.

For Mom, Woburn (Mass.)
High Class of 1952:
You were, in fact,
always a disc jockey.

Published by FFRW Press
Forestdale, MA
ISBN: 979-8-9930655-1-9 (paperback)
ISBN: 979-8-9930655-0-2 (digital online)
Library of Congress Control Number: 2025921405

First edition, December 1, 2025
Cover and interior design by Dana Collins

This is a work of nonfiction. Names, characters, businesses, places, events,
and incidents are presented as accurately as possible.
Printed in the United States of America

PROLOGUE:
LIFE IS A MIXTAPE

Singles remind me of kisses, albums remind me of plans. – Squeeze

Mixtapes remind me of everything. – Me

The math hurts. Try your best to not do the math.

So what if Tears for Fears released *Songs from the Big Chair* way back in February 1985, just in time for your senior prom? Your head *and* your heels are sure to ache if you keep reminding yourself that you've been swaying to "Head Over Heels" for forty plus years. It doesn't matter that *Talking Heads: 77* was released—wait for it—in 1977, just a few months after the original *Star Wars* movie hit the movie theaters. Yes, it was a very long time ago in a galaxy far, far away that "Psycho Killer" and so many of our other favorite new wave songs first came out.

So no, try not to do the math.

Instead, focus on the feelings.

Long before our adult selves found a therapist, our teenage selves found that "our music"—new wave, punk, alternative, post-punk, or whatever genre or sub-genre of alternative you call it—helped us make sense of our ever-changing moods. Somehow, alternative music temporarily eased the teenage anxiety we felt over anything and everything, and bands like Roxy Music and New Order and Violent Femmes sparked something inside of us that almost felt like confidence. And because we saw ourselves as being a *little* different from our "popular" classmates (because we were geeks, nerds, "drama fags" and so on), we found a much-needed sense of community when we discovered other geeks and nerds and drama fags who really liked this weird music, too. (Forgive the dated homophobic term "drama fag." It was a pretty common slur jocks used back in the '80s to belittle the kids who signed up for school plays. Little did they know that for a nerdy thirteen-year-old boy, school plays guaranteed quality time with thirteen-year-old girls. And the "cast parties" to celebrate a successful production? Total make-out fests.)

In high school, we didn't categorize ourselves as "disco"— Madonna, Michael Jackson, Whitney Houston and the like. Nor did we gravitate to the fist-pumping, latex-clad metal/hair bands—Quiet Riot, Mötley Crüe, Def Leppard. And we were getting kinda tired of our older siblings' music—Peter Frampton, ZZ Top, Led Zeppelin. In the late 1970s and early 1980s, we knew all the words to *those songs* from an unavoidable form of background radiation called "Top 40 radio." And on some level, we understood that the metalheads and burnouts and disco divas treasured *their* music to the same degree. But those songs didn't really speak to us. They didn't feel like *ours*.

And then one day we heard Ian Dury and the Blockheads singing "Hit Me With Your Rhythm Stick," or Devo urging us to "Whip It," or maybe the B-52's shouting in irrational harmony about something called a "Rock Lobster." And *things changed*.

The new wave/punk record collections we built with our precious disposable incomes, and the mixtapes we made with those records, were our audio Rorschach tests back then. They still are today. What emotional images did those songs conjure up when you first heard them thirty-five, forty or forty-five years ago? What do you see and hear and feel when you listen to those songs now?

Does a favorite song by Pet Shop Boys, R.E.M., the Pretenders, Squeeze, or the Cure take you *right back* to a very specific time and place? Is the journey back there sweet, or bitter?

Academic research has shown time and again that—for better or worse—music has a profound and measurable impact on a listener's emotional state—and even the very way the brain functions throughout the course of our long or short lives. Any of us who ever danced with abandon to INXS's "New Sensation" or cried ourselves to sleep listening to the Smiths' "Asleep" on repeat knows this is *fact*, even without access to the clinical data. Music helps us to remember, to forget, to feel good, to feel bad, and to feel like we're part of a community. With songs serious and silly and sad and weird, new wave, punk and post-punk music took us—and continues to take us—on a twisty-turny journey all over the emotional map.

Some of us have friends who know everything about sports, or cars, or that TV show *Friends*, or World War II; we're the people who know every word of the rap from Blondie's "Rapture." Gen X may be getting gray, but for us, new wave never gets old.

I've moved house a few times in the last couple of years, and for a while there I lost track of my beloved 1980s homemade mixtapes, many of which I had simply labeled "Those Songs." I wasn't particularly concerned about the possibility of losing access to the songs on those tapes; I still have a lot of them on vinyl, they stream on demand via "smart devices," and they even play over the PA system in the grocery store when we pop in for a box of fiber-enriched bran flakes.

No, I was upset that losing those mixtapes might forever erase the precious and emotionally packed memories they hold—as effectively as a magnet can erase a sixty-minute Memorex or a ninety-minute Maxell. Thankfully, many of those cassettes recently turned up in a mislabeled box in the new garage, the music and the memories intact. This book is about those mixtapes, and it's about the people, some long gone, who never fail to come to mind or back to life when those songs get replayed for the millionth time. This book is also about why those songs—*our* songs—often mean more to us today than they did "back in the day."

Just yesterday I stopped by the post office to buy some stamps, and the clerk noticed the address on the birthday card I was sending my son, Evan, who is (ouch, for me) turning thirty this year. The clerk, looking to be in her late fifties like me, smiled and asked: "Does he really live on Electric Avenue?" I confirmed that indeed he does.

And then, spontaneously and in perfect sync, we started singing that song about rockin' down to Electric Avenue, with our hilariously awful impressions of Eddie Grant.

We laughed, and she sighed a wistful sigh. "The eighties were the best," she said. "I wish I could go back."

Me too, nice postal lady. Me too.

So, let's go!

PART
1

BUT FIRST,
SOME PRE-PUNK MEMORIES

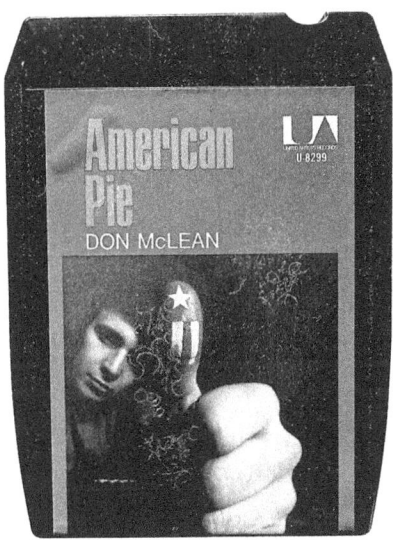

Chances are good your older brother had this 8-track tape in 1971.

IT'S OKAY. YOU CAN ADMIT that your favorite music wasn't always "alternative" and that your first pair of shoes weren't Doc Martens or Converse All-Stars. For many Gen Xers, music was simply called "AM radio," or "whatever our parents or older siblings were listening to while we tried to do our spelling homework." Sure, learning the difference between "your" and "you're" was very important (especially for us future social media posters), but the pop music from our 1970s childhoods taught us something far more lasting: those songs taught us how to *feel*.

When did you realize that those '70s songs were attacking your heart? One-hit wonder Morris Albert made the case for feeling all the feels when he reached number two on the charts in 1974 with "Feelings," a song that *whoa whoa whoa* you can no doubt sing from memory.

Me? I made the connection between music and emotions in 1973. That was the year that my second-grade music teacher, Miss D., seemed to be going through some serious shit.

Miss D. had remarkably shiny black hair, parted sharply down the middle just like Joan Baez, and it hung past the waistband of her super-groovy bell-bottom jeans. She was probably in her mid-twenties, her skin alabaster, her acoustic guitar almost as shiny as her hair. And, man, she must have had a horrible breakup that year.

One Thursday morning she taught me and my fellow seven-year-olds how to sing "I Am a Rock" (1966) by Simon and Garfunkel.

She'd tear up a little when she sang us the song, especially during the "I am an iiiiiiiisland" part and about the feelings that have died. She also taught us how to sing a teary version of that song about looking at clouds from both sides (now). Did I mention we were seven?

I wish I could have helped Miss D. back then. Perhaps I could have shown her some empathy by sharing my tales of woe about the playground bully or the sour milk in the school cafeteria. But I was immature and emotionally unavailable, and I still picked my nose on the regular. She was on her own.

More than fifty years later I sometimes think about Miss D., and I silently thank her for the maudlin musical education. Her struggle, whatever it was, likely set the sad-sack stage for my later love of bands like the Cure and the Smiths.

I bet Miss D. totally went goth in the 1980s.

Having learned about depression in music class, we'd then learn about anxiety in the media room, which was just down the hall from Miss D.'s tambourine-filled music room.

Once a week our class was ushered into this artificially darkened space, where we would watch 16mm film newsreels that kept us informed about "current events." It seemed like every week the newsreel included an update on the ongoing Strategic Arms Limitation Talks ("SALT II"), which sought to reduce the risk of nuclear war between the U.S. and the U.S.S.R. Our teacher would "joke" about how, when *he* was our age, he and his classmates had to perform "duck and cover" drills to prepare for the atomic doomsday his generation believed was imminent. "At least you don't have to duck and cover," he'd say, and the sharper seven-year-olds in the class knew he meant "because you're all going to melt instantly when it happens."

Every week, those newsreels featured the same old stock footage of intercontinental ballistic missiles launching in fiery slow-motion to an ominous voiceover about the rising tensions between the two global superpowers. I always felt an enormous sense of relief when the teacher rewound the film in real-time on-screen so we could watch the missiles fly in reverse, back into their silos. We were safe from Armageddon for at least another week.

It's little wonder we grew up to adore songs like Nena's "99 Red Balloons," Frankie Goes to Hollywood's "Two Tribes," Men at Work's "It's a Mistake," O.M.D.'s "Enola Gay," and Siouxsie and the

Banshees' "Cities in Dust." If we're gonna get nuked, we might as well get nuked with some cool music on in the background.

The 1970s, though, weren't all doom and gloom, and we had AM radio to soothe our anxious little souls. Today, when the emotionally overwrought Yacht Rock comes on the radio (and the wine and beer starts flowing), many of us fifty- or sixty-somethings are instantly transported back to those summer nights in 1972, or 1974 or 1976, when we waited for our favorite song to be played on the radio. We had our little black Radio Shack tape decks ready to capture the tunes that made us swoon, hoping the DJ wouldn't talk over the intro, or the end, and ruin the recording. Songs like "Cat's in the Cradle" by Harry Chapin (1974), "Sad Eyes" by Robert John (1979), and "Wildfire," by Michael Martin Murphey (1975).

In my grade-school opinion, Barry Manilow's "Mandy" (1974) and Looking Glass's "Brandy" (1972) were just plain dandy. But by 1982, in our too-cool-for-school young adult brains, we decided that these songs sucked. Deep down you know we loved them, though, and we still know every word to every song today. Don't believe me? Say "Alexa, play 'Yesterday Once More' by the Carpenters," (1971) and—*shooby doo lang lang*—watch what happens.

Music, memory and emotion are the ultimate three-piece band.

CALL IT WHAT YOU WILL

IT'S A TYPICAL SATURDAY morning over on Facebook, and thousands of Gen Xers of a certain musical persuasion are arguing over how to properly categorize the songs they loved so much back when they were teenagers—forty, forty-five years ago or more.

On community pages with tongue-twisting names like "70s & 80s New Wave and Post Punk (& Sub Genres) History and Music" (47,300 members), "New Wave UNITED 80's" (17,300 members), "Punk 77, New Wave Ska . . . and Now" (18,500 members), and "GenX Only" (with a whopping membership of 3 million and growing) you'll quickly see that no two Gen Xers look back on their alternative music-listening years the same way.

When did punk really begin, and when did it morph into new wave? Which bands qualify as post-punk, and which really should be labeled goth? Some of the richest interactions in these Facebook communities center on which of the big three musical mental filing cabinets—punk, new wave or post-punk—is the most appropriate place in which to sub-file the ska, pub rock, rockabilly and new romantic songs they loved so much in high school and college. The back and forth posting on these community pages sometimes reaches levels of religious fervor. These are the people who can name all fifty-two girls from that B-52's song about fifty-two girls.

You know – people like us.

I think we can all agree that any number of game-changing bands and one hit wonders are easy to categorize. Sex Pistols? Everyone concurs that Johnny Rotten and his mates are punk. A Flock of Seagulls, with that low-budget, tin foil-filled "I Ran" music video and that dude with the wildly asymmetrical haircut? Totally new wave.

But what about Talking Heads, who made our heads spin with *More Songs About Buildings and Food* (1978)? Are they punk? New wave? Post-punk? Does it even matter?

The distinction mattered—a lot—to Johnny Slash, briefly but memorably portrayed by Merritt Butrick in the short-lived 1982 high school-set CBS TV sitcom *Square Pegs*. In the school cafeteria, when a pre-Carrie Bradshaw Sarah Jessica Parker asks Johnny if he's "really" a punk rocker, he earnestly replies: "Punk? *No way*. I'm new wave. Totally different head . . . *totally*."

Square Pegs was way ahead of its time, or, at least, it was timed perfectly. While it aired for just a single season it faithfully captured the early-'80s high school experience with far more authenticity than any John Hughes movie could, and it featured guests like Devo and the Waitresses (who sang "I Know What Boys Like" in an episode about a school dance). Forget about HBO—this was peak TV! (Also, for a real cringe-inducing TV treat, go online and find the 1987 *ABC Afterschool Special* called "The Day My Kid Went Punk." You can thank me later.)

And what about acts like the Knack, the Cars, or U2? Were they new wave or—dare we say it—Top 40 pop? Well, yes to both, at one point or another in their careers.

I recently visited the Punk Rock Museum in Las Vegas to see if and how the curators there delineate the sometimes blurry boundaries between our favorite musical genres and subgenres. (Please note: you can get a tattoo and a cold beer when you visit the Punk Rock Museum, but you can't have a pop-up marriage ceremony there. The museum is just off the Vegas Strip, and with a late-'70s model stretch limousine parked out front that looks like it has a spiky mohawk haircut it's pretty hard to miss.)

Like a Hard Rock Cafe on steroids, the Punk Rock Museum is home to an expansive collection of musical memorabilia spanning decades, leaning heavily toward hardcore punk but inclusive (or at least tolerant) of us new wavers and post-punk romantics. Just a few artifacts on display: Joe Strummer's jacket and his 6-string guitar; a tower of late 1970s 8-track tapes by the Clash, Sex Pistols, Iggy Pop and Richard Hell; framed posters promoting concerts by the Gun Club ("Sex Beat"—great song!), Terry Hall from the Specials, Bauhaus, Mission of Burma and Green Day; a leather jacket and Gibson guitar belonging to Social Distortion's Jonny 2 Bags. Dee Dee Ramones's gold ring and padlock necklace are prominently displayed in a side-room that also houses a large collection of original handbills from the legendary 1970s alt/punk nightclubs CBGB and Max's Kansas City. A little bit of hardcore this, a little bit of new wave that.

So, call the music what you will. But now that we're sneaking up on fifty-five, sixty or more, maybe we should simply call all of our favorite '70s and '80s songs "classic alternative" and get back to our physical therapy routines. Of course, you're always welcome to jump onto Facebook and join the argument about what to call our music. Or you can just sit back and listen to the songs you liked back in the day—and absolutely treasure now.

WE ARE FAMILY

A bunch of Boomers (my siblings)
and me in the bowtie repping for Gen X.

SOMEWHERE BETWEEN THE LAUNCH of *Sputnik* (1957) and the tragic *Apollo 1* fire (1967), my mom and dad rocketed into the family way in a *big* way, having four kids in four years, then twins the next year, and then me four years later. That's a lot of groceries and earache medicine to finance, never mind servicing the mortgage, so they both worked eight days a week throughout the 1960s and 1970s. Long days in the city at the bank for Dad, suburban night jobs for Mom.

For a while, Mom worked nights as the receptionist at a gaudy wedding venue and "dinner theater" in Randolph, Massachusetts called the "Chateau de Ville," the fanciest-sounding thing I had ever heard of ever in my young life. Mom snuck some of my older siblings into the Chateau to see the Village People perform one night in 1977 or so. For years I lied and told people I went to that show, too. I did not. I was eleven, and it was way past my bedtime to be doing the "Y.M.C.A." dance.

I still remember the phone number I'd call to say goodnight to Mom—986-5000, no area code needed. To this day I think of that number whenever I hear Tommy Tutone sing "867-5309."

Our family of nine lived in a chocolate-brown "split-level raised ranch" in a fast food-pocked suburb just south of Boston, Massachu-setts, called Stoughton. If you squinted your eyes hard enough, our house looked a little like the iconic Brady Bunch house—perfect for a family of our size and last name. It was a home brimming with the stuff you'd expect to find in a 1970s house owned by a double-income post-War/Boomer family: a CB radio, lots of roller skates, mood rings for the girls, and a Pong video game system that was a "family present" for Christmas, 1975.

When she wasn't working, Mom was always home spinning her records—pre-disco Bee Gees, the Chicago Transit Authority, Jim Croce—burning those lyrics and those licks into our little brains for life. No one in our house played an instrument, but we sure played a lot of records. It's little wonder that in her 1952 yearbook entry, Mom wrote, daringly for the times, that her "HEART'S DESIRE" was "to become a woman disc jockey."

The music came from a coffin-shaped, hearse-sized faux-maple wood stereo console—a Zenith, maybe?—that had built-in speakers hidden behind brown cloth panels, a 33/45/78 turntable, and a bunch of shiny black knobs we weren't allowed to touch. In the low-ceil-inged family room, us kids would dance beneath a groovy painting of a Spanish guitar that teetered on the wall above a groovy orange couch. Mom had a beehive hairdo like Cindy Wilson from the B-52's.

On weekends, Dad's Boston-Irish brothers and sister would visit us in the 'burbs for a cookout—cold Michelob and Benson & Hedg-es "multifilter" cigarettes all around—and sing along with the *Irish Hit Parade* radio show (WROL 950 AM). Dad looked a bit like that TV detective Jim Rockford. His brothers, my uncles Jack and Dan-ny, would sing "Danny Boy," loud and proud and a little buzzed. Dad wasn't much for singing—or talking, to be honest—but boy could he hum along to an old-school Irish pub song. My too-many-to-count cousins and I would gallop around the patio dancing to that ridicu-lous but endearing "The Unicorn" song by the Irish Rovers, our little fingers wagging from our little foreheads. This Saturday afternoon ritual of Irish radio would prepare me for the invasion of Celtic rock-ers, like the Waterboys and the Pogues, that would come years later.

Meanwhile, my big brother JB had started amassing an impres-sive collection of 8-track tapes featuring artists like America, Don Maclean, and Bread. JB (Stoughton High School Class of '78) and I shared a basement bedroom with our other brother, Eddie (Stough-ton High Class of '79). JB and Eddie were six and five years older than me, respectively, and at the time they listened (non-stop) to what we now call "classic rock."

I loved when JB, sixteen years old in 1976 and me just ten, would drop the needle on one of his many Beatles albums, blasting the tunes through his four-foot tall, wood-paneled stereo speakers. (But that song about the number 9 scared me, as did the skunky smell of whatever they were smoking when my parents weren't home.) I wasn't wild about a lot of Eddie's music, though. He gravitated toward Bob Seger, Marshall Tucker and Lynyrd Skynyrd. JB painted the bedroom walls to look like the cover of Paul McCartney and Wings' 1974 album *Venus and Mars*—big yellow and red orbs joined by sharp-angled lines (Google it!), and the four 8x10 portraits of each Beatle that came with their self-titled "white" album looked down at us from the cheap wooden bifold closet doors.

Upstairs in their two shared bedrooms, my four sisters—Lisa (Stoughton High Class of '75), Maryellen (Stoughton High Class of '77) and Kathleen and Maureen ("the twins," Stoughton High Class of 1980) were listening to Carole King's *Tapestry* (1970), *The Best of Carly Simon* (1975), Fleetwood Mac's *Rumours* (1977) or Linda Ronstadt covering "You're No Good" (1974).

In 1979 (despite the recent Three Mile Island nuclear accident which reminded us that death by nuke could happen at any moment) our suburban family life—and our music—was simple, repeatable and predictable.

But life comes at you pretty fast, as Ferris Bueller warned us, and a few months later I learned that I would not be a member of the Stoughon High Class of 1984. Instead, the nine of us—the Grady Bunch—abruptly found ourselves living in a luxury apartment building high above Boston's waterfront, arguing with our parents over the merits of a band called the Clash.

BOSTON,
YOU'RE MY (NEW) HOME

The view from my new bedroom.

LET'S REWIND THIS MENTAL MIXTAPE to November 1980. I was fourteen years old and absolutely terrified of this big, noisy city called Boston, my new home. We'd moved here, to the heart of downtown in a high-rise called Harbor Towers, just eleven weeks earlier—me, Mom, Dad, my two brothers and my four sisters—from the very quiet suburb Stoughton, about thirty miles southwest of the city.

Dad had just gotten a big promotion at the bank, which was headquartered in the heart of Boston's Financial District, and he thought it might be nice to walk to work after years and years of going back and forth on the crowded commuter rail train, suburbs to city, city to suburbs, five days a week.

Mom landed a job as the manager of the gift shop at the Boston Tea Party Ships & Museum, just a half-mile away from our new apartment; there, she developed a real talent for selling commemorative spoons and little wooden boxes filled with tea to wide-eyed tourists and school kids on field trips. ("*Throw the tea—into the sea!*")

Mom and Dad were thrilled to be living "in town." But me? I was totally overwhelmed (paralyzed, really) by my new urban surroundings. Honking taxis! Strangers! Trash on the sidewalk! Parking meters! *Yikes*. In fact, I was pretty nervous about just stepping outside of the building.

Our new home was on the twenty-fourth floor, and every inch of the apartment had tall and wide windows that looked out at the city and the waterfront and the rusting elevated "Central Artery" highway below, crammed with traffic. These were alien landscapes to me, so very different from the quiet dead-end street we'd lived on back in the suburbs.

The sprawling three bedroom apartment—24F—was surrounded by tall office buildings that never seemed to turn their lights off at night. Airplanes coming to and from Logan Airport roared overhead around the clock. A few hundred feet from our towering cement building was its twin, another forty-story tower that, when seen together side by side, strike an iconic pose on Boston's skyline.

Like our tower, that one was filled with complete strangers, too. And not another kid in sight. The view afforded the occasional glimpse of an unknown neighbor—middle-aged, old, very old—dressing or undressing. We had uniformed door men who wore little black and blue hats, and the "moving on up to a de-lux apartment in the sky" theme from *The Jeffersons* was always ringing in my ears.

A public school kid my whole life, I was now just a few weeks into my freshman year at a private Catholic high school in the North End, Boston's "Little Italy," which I quickly learned you are absolutely not allowed to call it. The school, a pile of weathered bricks plopped just around the corner from the world-famous cannoli shop known as "Mike's Pastry," was filled with tough kids from every neighborhood in Boston: Tough Irish kids! Tough Italian kids! Tough Irish-Italian kids! And the teachers, Franciscan Friars in brown robes with white ropes around their waists (which they rejoiced in using for discipline), had all of us freshmen holding our breath. Even the lunchroom ladies terrified me. Our all-boys school had a dress code, and the cool kids wore skinny black neckties, like the guys from the Knack.

Borrowed from Dad's closet, my freshman year ties were wide. And plaid.

I missed my suburban friends, Gus and Bob. We were girl-crazy hetero when we met in middle school, but the jocks and burnouts called us "drama fags" because we happily performed in school plays. I sorely missed the soft-serve ice cream stand a short bike ride away from my old house in Stoughton, and I really missed the one-screen movie theater where, traumatically, I had seen *Jaws* in 1975 at the age of nine.

So when my big brother JB asked me one November night in 1980 if I wanted to take public transit—the MBTA Red Line—to see a new movie with him at the Harvard Square Theater, I was thrilled but super-anxious. The idea of descending into the subway—America's first underground transit system, built in 1901—scared the crap out of me. But I was fourteen, feeling lonely, and was elated to be asked to go *anywhere* with my way-cool older brother JB. Especially to a movie.

And so I said "yes" to a trip to *Times Square*. The movie, not the neighborhood.

My eyes and ears popped at what came on the screen and out of the theater loudspeakers.

The movie tells the timeless tale of two teenage runaways trying to make it as rockstars in New York City, and it starts with Roxy Music's "Same Old Scene" blasting over the opening credits. Hearing Bryan Ferry's high-end vocals contrasting with the low-end bass line in that song was transformative. And over the next 106 minutes I was happily exposed to a Chernobyl-level dose of new wave music, which I'd never really heard much of before but have been listening to ever since.

In the movie, a rich-kid teenage girl named Pamela Pearl lives with her evil politician dad in a fancy Manhattan high-rise—not too dissimilar from my new home in Harbor Towers. Sick of Dad's questionable ethics and frequent absences, Pamela runs away from home. After being captured and institutionalized by Dad's minions, Pamela meets her soulmate—Nicky Marotta—who is handcuffed to an adjacent bed in their shared room in a psych ward. Somehow, Pamela and Nicky escape, fleeing to the dirty old pre-Disneyfied mean streets of Times Square, where they set out to stick it to the man.

Pamela Pearl is played by Trini Alveredo, who later played Meg in the 1994 film version of *Little Women*, with Susan Sarandon (who dated David Bowie in the '80s). Nicky Marotta is played by Robin Johnson, who, for the longest time I mistakenly thought was the same person as Suzie Quatro, a.k.a., Leather Tuscadero from the TV show *Happy Days*. My bad. But Suzie *did* have a song on the *Times Square* soundtrack album.

But I digress.

Anyway, in the movie, an alternative-rock radio DJ played by Tim Curry (that sweet transvestite from Transsexual, Transylvania in *The Rocky Horror Picture Show*, and for you youngsters, the voice of Nigel Thornberry from the Nickelodeon cartoon *Wild Thornberries*) soon becomes an on-air patron to the rebellious duo of Pamela and Nicky. The runaways experiment with shoplifting, anti-establishment graffiti and spontaneous sidewalk-dancing with people of color while Curry spins some amazing new wave music in the background.

Later in the movie, with the help of DJ Curry, the girls—still eluding daddy and the authorities—manage to get time in a recording studio. They record their new alienation/protest songs, including the overly-rhymey "Damn Dog" and the surprisingly profane-for-its-time "Your Daughter is One." They quickly become punk-folk heroes known as "The Sleez Sisters," and then Nikki has a nervous breakdown in the rain.

Intense!

The soundtrack read like a who's who of our future mixtapes: Pretenders' "Talk of the Town," Roxy Music's "Same Old Scene"—each was a shot of audio adrenaline I hadn't known I needed. The Cure's "Grinding Halt," Talking Heads' "Life During Wartime" and Patti Smith's "Pissing in a River" . . . It felt like a secret world opening up, one bassline at a time. This was not a Barry Manilow album or the Little River Band on WRKO 680 AM. No, this music felt *important*, even if the movie itself was kinda goofy.

A few days later, I worked up the nerve to venture beyond the perimeter of my double high-rise apartment complex and sought out the *Times Square* soundtrack—double vinyl!—at the Harvard Coop record and bookstore on Devonshire Street in Boston. No luck. Eventually, I did find a copy at the Woolworth's in Boston's Downtown Crossing, of all places. And I still have it, and treasure it, here in the twenty-first century.

In his two-star review, film critic Roger Ebert wrote: "Of all the bad movies I've seen recently, (*Times Square*) is the one that projects the real sense of a missed opportunity . . . of potential achievement gone wrong."

Roger Ebert was right: It's not a great film. But it's a timeless record, and it made an ever-lasting impression on me.

Or as Roxy Music sang during the movie's opening credits: "It's still that same old movie that's haunting me."

A CLASH OVER THE CLASH

IT'S DECEMBER 8, 1980, a few weeks after my visit to *Times Square*— the movie, not the tourist trap—and during his "Monday Night Football" broadcast Howard Cosell informs the world that John Lennon has just been shot and killed in New York City. We're all devastated: we grew up with the Beatles "always on" in the background, just like everyone else on Earth. But my brother JB takes the news especially hard; it's the first time I remember ever seeing him cry. It was an angry cry.

It's almost Christmas, and Lennon's lovely "War is Over" plays in every store and on every radio station over and over again for the next few weeks. You didn't have to be a sophisticated adult like my older brothers and sisters to know that this is the end of a musical era. And under our family Christmas tree, two perfectly flat and perfectly square presents would soon present further evidence that our family (and the rest of the world, apparently) was at a musical crossroad.

Mom, our would-be DJ, understood how important music was to all of her kids, especially to JB. So for a "family Christmas present" she had discreetly ventured to the Strawberries Records & Tapes store in Downtown Boston to buy us seven kids two new albums: *The River*, by Bruce Springsteen, and *Sandinista!* by the Clash.

A double album that would quickly go gold, *The River* sounded like everything my sibs and I listened to back in the 'burbs. It was fine—"Hungry Heart," "Cadillac Ranch," "I'm A Rocker" and all that. But the three-album (!!!) *Sandinista!* grabbed fourteen of our collective eighteen ears by the throat, with tracks like "Police On My Back," "The Call Up" and "The Magnificent Seven" mesmerizing and captivating us kids.

Mom and Dad were pleased with the Christmas joy their two vinyl presents had brought, especially given the pall that had fallen over the house after Lennon's murder, but they soon realized they weren't exactly big fans of the Clash. JB had the albums *Sandinista!* and *London Calling* in heavy rotation on our bedroom hi-fi for months on end in late 1980 and into the new year. One morning in 1981 Mom confronted JB, Eddie and me as we were all preparing for the day ahead: "I know the words to that song you keep playing, and it's disgusting," she hissed, before slamming our bedroom door shut behind her.

After a quick a huddle, we three brothers concluded that Mom was referring to the track "Death Or Glory" from *London Calling*, which featured some pretty provocative f-word-laden lyrics about sex, nuns and the Catholic Church.

Mom sort of had a point, I guess.

But, man, that song (as the kids say these days) is a "banger."

THE WALL

ONE NIGHT IN 1982, JB inexplicably scrawled the words "Lust Kills" in black magic marker on our bedroom wall.

Even after Mom painted over them, you could still sort of see the words bleeding through.

SCARED OF THE POLICE

AFTER *SANDINISTA!*, THE MUSIC THAT was always on in our house started to sound *different*: a little less Olivia Newton-John, a little more Pretenders. It wasn't long before my twin sisters wore out the extended 12-inch version of "Tainted Love/Where Did Our Love Go" (1981) by Soft Cell and the Human League's *Dare* (1981) album. Mary Ellen came home one day with a copy of "Jet Boy, Jet Girl," a scandalous 1978 single from Elton Motello. (Google those lyrics if you can't recall the song. *Wow!*) And I remember my oldest sister, Lisa, really liking that Blondie song "Heart of Glass" (1978).

All seven of us were constantly bopping around the apartment listening to "Enola Gay" (1981) by O.M.D. on repeat.

On January 15, 1982 my sisters were gathering up their neon hair scrunchies and taffeta skirts to get ready to see the Go-Go's open for the Police at the sweaty old Boston Garden, home of the Boston Celtics, the Boston Bruins, and the occasional Disney on Ice show. This was the tour where the Go-Go's *Beauty and the Beat* album surpassed Sting and company's *Ghost in the Machine* on the Billboard Hot 100 chart, much to the surprise of both acts.

My sisters would end up having a blast at the show, but I was still too anxious about city living to brave an actual live concert at a big stadium. It was one thing to raid JB's growing collection of punk and new wave albums to make my own mixtapes in the safety of our shared bedroom. And tentatively exploring the Downtown Crossing record shops just a few streets away was another. But going to a live concert was a bridge too far for this raised-in-the-burbs fifteen-year-old. I spent almost every weekend back in the familiar environs of my hometown, Stoughton, sleeping over at my friends' houses. Funny how "generalized anxiety disorder" first appeared in the third edition of the American Psychiatric Association's *Diagnostic and Statistical Manual of Mental Disorders*, or "*DSM-III*," in 1980, the same year I moved to the city. The *DSM-III* describes 265 unique mental disorders—almost exactly one for every weekday of the year.

Today, I still kick myself for being too anxious to have skipped that concert, where I could have seen firsthand if the Go-Go's really had the beat and if every little thing the Police do really is magic.

Eventually I noticed that my brother JB had found work as a security guard at the Orpheum in Boston, a 2,600-seat theater hidden at the end of a narrow, dirty alley near the Boston Common. The Orpheum was just one city block beyond the Woolworth's where a few months earlier I'd found the *Times Square* soundtrack, but it was still too far from our apartment for my comfort. Having only just started to dip my toes into new wave music, I didn't appreciate the significance of JB's new position of authority in the world of rock and roll.

Concerts I should have asked JB to sneak me into in 1981 included Ultravox opening for U2, and the Boomtown Rats. I'll fight to the death to protect JB's bootleg cassette recording of that November 14, 1981 U2 concert.

In 1982, I should have asked my big brother to smuggle me in to see the Pretenders for at least one of their three shows that January. Or Stray Cats in April. I could have even seen Asia sing "Heat Of The Moment" at the Orpheum later that year. (I still have the single today. No, it's not new wave. Yes, I bought it at Woolworth's.) I had no idea until recently that the Clash played there on September 8, 1982, and that my brother worked the door that night.

"Should I stay or should I go?" Dammit, I shoulda went!

I finally clued into the fact that JB's wrinkly blue uniform and tin security badge could open some very cool backstage doors for me, if I asked nicely and if I could work up the courage to actually go. On February 18, 1983, JB snuck me into my very first "real" concert. I was sixteen years old, and Phil Collins was promoting his new album *Hello, I Must Be Going!*. A terrific show then, a terrific album still today. (Though he's not particularly new wave, Phil Collins, as far as I am concerned, can do no wrong. Save for "Sussudio.")

My persistent suburbia-versus-city anxiety momentarily overcome, I made it to and through my first concert, unscathed and delighted. And I soon realized that, hello, I must be going, too: going to a lot more live shows from now on, that is.

Five years later—April 29, 1988 to be exact—I told Mom I was going to a concert at the Orpheum. JB wasn't working there any more, and she looked worried.

"Be careful," she whispered. "The guy on the news said that 10,000 maniacs are going to be there tonight."

ROCK THIS (SMALL) TOWN

*My good friend Gus, forever 21 in the cover photo
of this 1986 mixtape.*

BACK IN STOUGHTON my one-year-older-than-me buddies
Bob and Gus had somehow gotten their drivers' licenses. I'd take
the commuter train (Dad's old Monday–Friday train) from Boston
to spend almost every weekend meandering about the suburbs in
Gus's dads' big blue 1960-something Ford Fairlane. A clunky D-battery-powered boombox was always blasting from the backseat, and
I was regularly raiding JB's record collection to make my own mixtapes for myself and my two best friends.

When *you* made someone a mixtape back in the '80s, did you
write the names of each song and artist on the little cardboard case
insert? (I only recently learned that this little piece of paper is called
a J-card.) Did you draw elaborate designs with your toxic multi-colored magic markers for the case? From my second mixtape on, I
never included any information about what was on them, thinking
that half the fun was the surprise emotional journey you hoped the
mix would take the listener on. I would, however, always name my
tapes something random and pretentious, like "Tunes to Tan By, Vol.
42," in a teenage effort to be quirky and cool. And to the plastic case
I would always add a photo, cut to fit.

My good friend Bob, 1983-ish.

Also, when I made a mixtape, I always made sure to use my teeth to pry out the two little black tabs located on the far end of the top of a blank cassette. Doing this meant the recipient of your musical gift couldn't record over the mix you had lovingly curated for them, unless they put some adhesive tape over the holes. (In the 1980s, taping over a gifted mixtape was the ultimate betrayal.)

Of course, four decades later, I still have the very first mixtape I made exclusively for those girlfriendless nights out in the car with my pals Gus and Bob.

What's on the tape? Some cool new songs the three of us were just starting to learn the words to:

"Rock the Casbah / Should I Stay or Should I Go," The Clash
"Sex & Drugs & Rock & Roll," Ian Dury
"Love Plus One," Haircut One Hundred
"Goody Two Shoes," Adam and the Ants
"Stepping Out," Joe Jackson
"Where's Captain Kirk?," Athletico Spizz 80
"Who Can It Be Now?," Men at Work
"Stray Cat Strut," The Stray Cats

For some reason, I had also squeezed Elton John's "Funeral for a Friend/Love Lies Bleeding" onto the mixtape, at the very end of side 1. "Funeral" is a wonderful rollercoaster of a song from 1973 that clocks in at just over eleven minutes, and the first half is a long, dirge-like instrumental. A classic, for sure. But coming on in the car right after the Stray Cats did their strut, that ten-year-old Elton song creaked and croaked like Peter Brady's voice in the recording studio with the Silver Platters. *"When it's time to change, you've got to rearrange . . ."*

The mix of songs on that tape is near-perfect musical study of early-'80s puberty.

Bob was working after school in the deli at the local supermarket, so he always changed the lyrics to our favorite Clash song when we sang along in the car:

It's always cheese, cheese, cheese
You're happy when I'm on my knees
I slice it thin you want it fat
I wish that you'd get off my back
Well come on and let me know
Turkey breast or chicken roll

We thought we were pretty damned cool. Stoughton, my humble little hometown, became the unlikely epicenter of a fierce and well-publicized national debate over the First Amendment and pornography in 1982, when an adult bookstore suddenly opened its sticky little doors in the middle of downtown. It was called The Times Square Bookstore, of course. Thousands of protestors from across the U.S. rallied outside the building everyday, and one night Frank Reynolds, anchor of the ABC Evening News, broadcast live from outside the bookstore.

Someone behind him held up a sign that read "You're a Nut if You Like Smut."

Gus and Bob and I were sixteen, seventeen years old, so of course we liked smut. The dirty bookstore was just a few hundred feet from the train station that Gus and Bob would pick me up at on my weekend visits back, and to annoy the protestors we'd crank the volume on the backseat boombox as we drove by. "Sex and drugs and rock and roll . . ."

Gus and I expanded our musical education that year thanks to a little name-that-tune quiz game that Bob invented. The three of us would cram into Bob's bedroom and we'd surround his record player, Pepsis in hand. Bob would then spin ten or fifteen seconds of a song before pulling up the tone arm.

With our backs to the turntable, Gus and I would have to guess the artist and the name of the song. Bonus points if we could name the album. This was a terrific way to waste time on a snowy suburban night in the pre-social media 1980s.

Bob dropped the needle one night on a song that was relatively new to us, and very quickly I shouted, "that's 'I'm Special,' by the Pretenders!"

"No!" Bob faux-raged, as if I had committed the most vile of sins. "The proper song title is 'Brass in Pocket!' from their self-titled 1979 album *Pretenders*! Jeezzzus what is wrong with you?!"

These days, that song comes up on the SiriusXM 1st Wave channel display with both—"Brass in Pocket (I'm Special)." I take great joy in pointing this out to Bob whenever we're in the car together and this song comes on. We're petty like that, because these things are important.

During our name-that-tune game sessions in 1982, Bob would play snippets of deep tracks from Squeeze, Graham Parker, Elvis Costello, and on and on it went, with me and Gus successfully identifying half the songs and committing to memory the names of the ones we got wrong. Bob also snuck more than a few ten- or fifteen-second snippets from Bob Dylan's *Blood on the Tracks* into his guessing game, which seemed out of place compared to the very British music we were feasting on back then. I soon learned that Bob was a closet Dylan bootleg collector. Years and years later he got married and named his first kid "Dylan," and years and years later I still adore that album, and his son.

Bob and Gus and I were thick as thieves throughout the 1980s, and still are today, despite the many miles between us and the obligations of family and work. We still talk about the weekend we watched the 1985 *Live Aid* broadcast, in a soda- and junk food-filled basement at Bob's house. We were so excited to see Elvis Costello play at *Live Aid*, waiting hours for his performance, and we couldn't help but feel disappointed when he took to the stage and sang just one song, "All You Need Is Love," by The Beatles.

I mean—great song, great rendition, but . . . just one three-minute song? Gus and Bob and I overcompensated the following year when the three of us slept overnight in the alley outside the Orpheum to be first in line to buy tickets to Elvis's three-night "Spectacular Spinning Songbook / Costello Sings Again" tour.

A few years later still, Gus got married and named his first born "Nick," cheerfully reminding me and Bob that "Nick's your buddy. Nick's your pal. Nick's the kinda guy you can trust, the kinda guy you can drink a beer with."

That's a line we repeated a lot from the 1985 movie *The Sure Thing*, starring John Cusack, who happens to be my very special birthday buddy.

A BRIEF EXCURSION DOWN THE JOHN CUSACK RABBIT HOLE

Spot the difference: Mr. Cusack and me.

JOHN CUSACK WAS BORN on June 28, 1966.

So was I.

I like to think this isn't a coincidence.

Mr. Cusack, after all, is the patron saint of the cassette mixtape, thanks to his many music-themed movies, and here I am professing my undying love for that sacred audio format in this silly book.

Mr. Cusack is a well-known fan of the Clash, and the Clash helped me with my daunting high school Spanish homework via their hit "Should I Stay or Should I Go": "Esta indecisión me molesta . . . si no quieres, líbrame . . . Dígame! ¿Qué tengo ser?"

We have so much in common.

In his 2000 hipster masterpiece *High Fidelity*, Mr. Cusack plays Rob Gordon, the emotionally stunted owner of a used record shop who arranges his enormous album collection alphabetically, then chronologically, and, when depressed, "autobiographically."

I arrange my albums, too. Sort of. Well, they're shelved.

In *High Fidelity*, Rob and his wacky record store friends—Dick (perfectly played by a low-key Todd Louiso) and Barry (an unforgettably manic Jack Black)—constantly try to one-up each other with their carefully curated mixtapes and their mastery of musical trivia. Much like my two best friends, Gus and Bob.

In the 1989 movie *Say Anything . . .*, Mr. Cusack's character, Lloyd Dobbler, iconically holds a cassette boombox high over his head, blasting Peter Gabriel's "In Your Eyes" outside of the house of the girl he pines for, class valedictorian Diane Court. Diane's character is played by the wonderfully named Ione Skye, whose real-life dad is the 1960s folk singer Donovan, who played an Amnesty International concert with Phil Collins in 1981.

Phil Collins, as you may recall, was my first concert, so there's that incredibly strong connection between Mr. Cusack and myself, as well.

In late 1982, our family moved out of our Harbor Towers apartment (it had suddenly "gone condo") and into a shiny new high-rise rental apartment complex just next to Boston's Old State House. We had *two* apartments there, in that sleek gray and black tower with the fancy name: the Devonshire. Mom and Dad (and sometimes my two brothers) and I were holed up in apartment 2005, on the twentieth floor.

Six floors down, my sisters were always coming and going from their little apartment, number 1408.

Did you know that in 2007 John Cusack starred in a film called *1408*? Of course he did.

Now, please don't tell my sisters, but when they were all away one weekend sometime in the mid-1980s I reached a certain significant "romantic milestone" in apartment 1408. The Thompson Twins' "Hold Me Now" was playing on my battery operated boombox, and at 4 minutes 44 seconds, that song was just the right length for the teenage effort underway.

Well, maybe a minute or two too long, in truth.

Back in 2023, before I quit Twitter because it had become a haven for neo-Nazis, I posted a link to a blog I'd written about my one-sided relationship with Mr. Cusack.

He "liked" it!

John Cusack ✔ liked your Tweet
have a slice of parasocial birthday
cake with me and @johncusack.
thosesongs.blog/2023/06/28/
the... pic.twitter.com/
XKIDxPBBhL

SUDDENLY LAST SUMMER

Cover photo from a MASP mixtape.
I'm hiding, first row, second from left.

IT'S SUMMER 1983, AND I'M one of about 150 high school juniors from across Massachusetts spending the summer at Milton Academy, a prestigious private boarding school just south of Boston. This is the Massachusetts Advanced Studies Program, and we are "MASS-Pees," sixteen- and seventeen-year old kids who get to live here for six weeks in what amounts to a trial run for whatever overpriced college is probably in our future.

Milton Academy's campus looks like a miniature Harvard Yard, and—unlike our friends back home looking for jobs at the South Shore Plaza or playing Pac-Man at the local Papa Gino's—we are working our way through two college-level courses every day for half a day. Our teachers are accomplished astronomers, noted journalists and former politicians. Our graduate student resident-assistants, all of whom hail from Ivy League schools, keep telling us that they are very accomplished, too. We are this summer's chosen few, the smartest kids in the state who ever applied to this particular program this particular year, and we think we're pretty cool.

Well, I think *everyone else* is pretty cool.

All the girls are Molly Ringwald cute, and most of the guys, despite being academic overachievers back home, are also super-confident lacrosse players who don't think twice about taking off their sleeveless T-shirts while playing frisbee on the manicured quad. I am surrounded by Jake after Jake after Jake from *Sixteen Candles*.

But me? I'm dealing with a measurable level of anxiety about my right to even be here. I'm struggling in my astronomy class, unable to correctly weigh the moon using the astro-mathematical formula provided by our world-famous teacher. I haven't caught the attention of a single Molly look-alike yet. And there's no way I'm taking my shirt off during frisbee sessions with the guys: back acne and teenage man-boobs can have that effect on a young man's confidence.

The good people at the Gillette razor company have given me a scholarship to attend this exclusive program based on my eleventh grade report card, and while I'm only shaving once or twice a week at this point I don't want to let them down. But my anxiety is spiking.

Good thing I have my trusty Sanyo cassette tape boombox and my "special coping music."

If you were a certain kind of bookish new wave-leaning nerd back in the early 1980s, chances are that you sought out your fair share of "artsy" movies—especially if you were lucky enough to have a cinema nearby that played such things. Sure, midnight showings of *The Rocky Horror Picture Show* were a rite of passage for so many in Gen X, but do you remember those small indy movies like *Stranger Than Paradise* (1984) and *Repo Man* (1984), with their classical/jazz/punk/bizarro soundtracks? So good.

For this anxious, not-particularly-popular high school student, the Harvard Square Cinema had become an important friend in recent years. While the cool group of my classmates would spend their Saturdays at "all ages" punk concerts at the nasty old Channel Club in South Boston, seeing bands like Gang Green and Black Flag, I'd be sitting with myself in the dark at the Harvard Square Theater, nibbling on popcorn during a "$7 Saturday double feature" of artsy flicks. This was the theater where JB had taken me to see *Times Square* that ear-awakening night in November 1980, and it regularly featured movies with amazing instrumental and operatic soundtracks. Movies like *Diva* (1981) *Gallipoli* (1981), and *Das Boot* (1982), their soundtracks stuffed with classical music and opera and packing quite an emotional punch. Thanks to the composer Vangelis, we had movies like *Blade Runner* (1982), *Chariots of Fire* (1981) and *The Year of Living Dangerously* (1982) that were blending futuristic synthesizers with surprising orchestral maneuvers to produce a new, seductive sound.

This movie-music genre became my "special coping music," a cassette-based alternative to the yet-to-be-invented Prozac, and I'd soon be scouring the used record store bins for soundtracks to these and other films to complement my little collection of Men at Work and the Fixx singles. (Of course, being raised on Bugs Bunny reruns back in the 1970s meant I had already developed a fondness for Ruffini and Verdi and Wagner. "The Rabbit of Seville?" "What's Opera, Doc?" Now *that's* what I call music, too!)

But I digress.

A few weeks into the MASP program, I call home (collect) from the rotary payphone in the lobby of my ivy-covered dorm building. Mom tells me that Channel 56—a local UHF TV station best known for the *Creature Double Feature with Dale Dorman* program on Saturdays—has been calling our house.

It seems that my years-old membership in the station's *"Star Trek* Fan Club" finally qualifies me to host an upcoming rerun of *Star Trek* on TV.

Can I be there this weekend to videotape my introduction?

You bet I can!

And so, two weeks later and just a few nights before our little academic sleep-away camp will come to an end, a large crowd of Mollys and Jakes are crammed around the wood-paneled console TV in the lobby of my dorm. They are there to watch my broadcast TV debut.

As word gets around that I will be on TV, I somehow acquire a nickname. It's the first nickname I have ever had in my life, and it's a cool one at that: "Shady Grady." 6 p.m. arrives, and there I am on screen, feathered Scott Baio hair and all, describing how "the Enterprise crew encounters a race of mysterious aliens whose plight is hard for humans to understand" or something like that, "until Mr. Spock, of all people, teaches Kirk and the crew a lesson in empathy."

Star-struck and camera shy, I had no idea what I was saying when I read the cue cards in front of the Channel 56 cameras a few weeks ago, and now I am dying inside as my tanned and talented summer classmates watch the broadcast. On the small, square TV screen, I'm a pimply-faced goofball wearing a purple "Channel 56 Star Trek Club" T-shirt, my unmuscular arms extra pale from all those long-sleeved frisbee games.

I am on TV talking about alien space stuff in the most sincere and earnest way possible.

And when I'm done with my episode intro, and after the U.S.S. *Enterprise* whooshes across the opening credits, my classmates cheer. They actually cheer! For the short remainder of the summer program, I'm greeted and treated like a star in the little bubble we inhabit on campus.

After laying low for three years or so to get a handle on my "we-live-in-the-city-now" anxiety, it felt good to be in the spotlight. Really good.

On move-out day I pack my Arthur C. Clarke paperbacks and my Maxell mixtapes and my Sanyo boombox and head home to the Devonshire with Mom and Dad, knowing that I learned *something* this summer: the power of mass media to turn a nobody into a somebody.

Who cares that I flunked astronomy? The space aliens on TV had made me popular for seventy-two hours.

It's been forty plus years since that summer and every now and then I come across the first mixtape I made for myself when I got home after MASP ended. The tape itself broke a long time ago, twisting around the heads of a cheap boombox. But I kept the storage case, which features a (now fading) picture of me and all the guys from my dorm at that summer program. The songs from that playlist are long gone, but holding the case itself is a powerful reminder that, for a fleeting moment, I was once a Jake from *Sixteen Candles* too.

A few weeks later, in September 1983, a mixtape arrived in the mail, sent from one of my MASP classmates.

What's on it? Some O.M.D., Tommy Tutone, Transvision Vamp (!), Psychedelic Furs, and a whole lot of R.E.M.'s *Murmur* album. Bonus tracks: a bunch of back-to-back songs from Trio—the German synth band whose "Da Da Da" song was made mainstream-famous in a 1999 Volkswagen TV ad. If memory serves, the summer classmate who made the tape was named Bill, and he was a big fan of R.E.M. Later, I heard he'd started an R.E.M. tribute band called Deep in Sleep. He was so damned cool, I thought back then. And still do, now.

I'd look him up if I could only remember his last name.

It has been a while.

A MILLION MILES AWAY

The view from apartment 2005, July 4, 1985.

LIKE HARBOR TOWERS, THE forty-two-story Devonshire (our family's new home) felt a million miles away from Stoughton and my friends there, Gus and Bob. And just like at Harbor Towers, there were no kids anywhere close to my age at the Devonshire.

I did, however, get to ride in the elevator with a weirdly random collection of 1980s celebrities.

Marvelous Marvin Hagler, the boxer who reigned mightily as the undisputed middleweight champion from 1980 to 1987, briefly had an apartment there. Mr. Marvelous grew up in Brockton, Massachusetts, the rough and tumble city that borders my hometown of Stoughton. I didn't know much about boxing so I had little to say whenever our paths crossed in the lobby or on the lift. Maybe I should have told him how I'd purchased my very first LP—the *Star Wars* soundtrack—at the Bradlees at Westgate Mall in Brockton when I was eleven years old. Surely Marvin and I could have successfully bonded over shared Westgate Mall memories. But I was too scared to even look at him whenever we got on the elevator together. All those muscles, and me so scrawny.

I took a part time job in the tiny (and I mean *tiny*) newsstand/ coffee shop in the lobby of the building. One 1985-ish Sunday morning, while I was brewing the coffee and assembling the Sunday papers, Steven Tyler, the legendarily manic frontman from Aerosmith, stopped by. Rumor had it that he'd taken an apartment at the Devonshire, but I had yet to see him on the elevator, and the doormen were mum. That morning, I was playing my cassette copy of the Beatles' *Abbey Road* on my little boombox that was tucked in next to the cash register. When he heard the music, Mr. Tyler shrieked *"yeah, yah, my man, that's some good music!"* in the way that only Steven Tyler can shriek.

It was 8 a.m. and, yes, he was adorned in many multi-colored scarves.

Mr. Tyler purchased a pack of cigarettes, a travel-size package of Q-tips, a container of Vaseline, a copy of *Playboy*, and was quickly on his way. In a small, awkward, and pornographically Beatle-esque way, I think he and I bonded in that very moment—although he never did introduce me to his daughter Liv, who would steal the hearts of an entire generation of teenage boys with her appearance in the 1995 record store-set movie *Empire Records*. (Liv must have been seven or eight years old in the mid-1980s, so I guess I can forgive him.)

Years later, deep into my outsized Elvis Costello obsession, I would learn that the well-dressed English lady who never smiled at me on the Devonshire elevator was Angela Rippon, the BBC newsreader who inspired Elvis's song "Green Shirt" from his 1979 *Armed Forces* album. If you know the song, I feel compelled to tell you that Ms. Rippon did not tease or flirt with me, nor did she shine all the buttons on her green shirt when we rode the lift together on occasion.

Jim Belushi was in town performing in a play at a nearby theater, and he'd taken an apartment at the Devonshire for the duration of that engagement. This was less than a year after his brother John died from a heroin overdose. Since 1975, John Belushi had been a staple in the bedroom I shared with my two brothers, as we had a little black and white TV next to JB's record player and we watched *Saturday Night Live* almost every weekend—way past my bedtime.

I stepped into the elevator one afternoon and there was Jim Belushi. I recognized him immediately from his stint on the short-lived TV show *Working Stiffs* from 1980.

Never one to leave an awkward silence silent, I awkwardly offered my condolences about the loss of John.

"I couldn't possibly imagine losing a big brother," I told him. Not that he asked.

Just a few years later I wouldn't have to imagine.

FOR THE RECORD

IF YOU DIDN'T HAVE A BIG BROTHER like JB to expose you to new wave music through an ever-expanding record collection, you always had *Saturday Night Live*, featuring John Belushi and so many other comedic legends. From 1975 to 1989, *SNL* both reflected and drove the growing popularity of punk and new wave artists. Season 1, in 1975, had plenty of our parents' favorite singers as musical guests—Neil Sedaka, Desi Arnaz Jr., and Paul Simon (three times in just twenty-four episodes!). But on April 17, 1976 *SNL* put the spotlight on the Patti Smith Group, which performed "Gloria" and a raucous cover of the Who's "My Generation." *SNL* Season 2 featured performances by James Taylor, Paul Simon again, and Leo Sayer (of "You Make Me Feel Like Dancin'" fame), but proto-punks the Kinks and alt-folkie Joan Armatrading also got some airtime that season.

Paul Simon sang again in Season 3, but a few weeks later, on December 17, 1977, Elvis Costello and the Attractions made nerdy new wave history on the *SNL* stage. Elvis was supposed to sing "Less Than Zero," a funky but nonetheless slow- to mid-tempo track from his debut album, *My Aim is True*. As any new wave fan who ever contemplated buying a ticket for one of those 1980s nostalgia cruises knows, Elvis played a few bars of "Less Than Zero" before abruptly stopping the music. Looking directly into the live camera, Elvis—scrawny in his too-tight suit and his oversized Buddy Holly eyeglasses—said: "I'm sorry ladies and gentleman, there's no reason to do this song here." He then launched into "Radio, Radio," from his forthcoming album *This Year's Model*. This act of musical insurrection infuriated *SNL* showrunner and famously freaky control-freak Lorne Michaels, and for years legend had it that Costello was banned from the show for life.

SNL Seasons 4 and 5 brought Devo, Kate Bush, Talking Heads, the B-52's, Gary Numan, the Specials and Blondie into unsuspecting American homes. (Heck, Debbie Harry was even a guest on *The Muppet Show* in January, 1981, helping Kermit the Frog's nephew Robin earn his "Punk Merit Badge" from his Frog Scout troop. Punk was definitely leaning into the mainstream for a while there.)

Before the 1980s closed out, more than a few of our favorite alternative acts appeared on *SNL*, signaling that our music had arrived. The Clash. Men At Work. David Bowie. Duran Duran. Dexy's Midnight Runners. Eddie Grant. Stray Cats. Big Country. The Motels. Adam Ant, the Fixx, Madness and Thompson Twins. Also, Frankie Goes to Hollywood, Simple Minds, the Dream Academy, the Cult, Joe Jackson, Laurie Anderson, Level 42, and E.G. Daily (famous to us Gen Xers from her appearances in the movies *Valley Girl*, *Pee-wee's Big Adventure* and *Better Off Dead*, starring the ever-present John Cusack).

And don't forget about the *SNL* episodes that featured Buster Poindexter, Ric Ocasek, the Pretenders, Paul Young, the Cars, Eurhythmics, Suzanne Vega, Los Lobos, Sting, Bryan Ferry, Simply Red, 10,000 Maniacs, the Sugar Cubes, Edie Brickell & New Bohemians, Tracy Chapman, the Bangles, Cowboy Junkies, Living Colour, David Byrne and k.d. lang.

They even let Elvis Costello come back in 1988.

Speaking of Elvis, back in the late 1970s, he had a brief but intense affair with English model Bebe Buell, who is the biological mother of Liv Tyler with Aerosmith's Steven Tyler. At the time of Liv's birth, the Aerosmith singer was too strung out on, well, *everything*, to parent. So Bebe and singer/producer Todd Rundgren raised Liv together until Liv met Steven in the late '80s. Todd Rundgren (famed for the 1973 hit song "Hello It's Me") would go on to produce *Skylarking*, the groundbreaking 1986 album by XTC famous for its track "Dear God." I first got my hands on *that* record when my Devonshire coffee shop/newsstand manager Jeff—a nine-fingered banjo player—made me a cassette copy. I played that Maxell to death while working weekend shifts, waiting for the next random celebrity to stop by for Q-tips and Vaseline.

JB loved that XTC album, too.

But I digress.

My point is—"alternative" music was everywhere in the early and mid 1980s, featured front and center on TV shows like *Miami Vice* and in movies like *Valley Girl* and *Pretty in Pink*. Each new release was eagerly anticipated, with the cool kids waiting in line at the record store to get their hands on the Smiths's debut album *The Smiths*, R.E.M.'s sophomore release *The Reckoning* or U2's *War*.

Mom came home from work on April 27, 1983, with a copy of the B-52's' *Whammy!* on cassette, an early birthday gift for me that she picked up on her lunch hour at Strawberry's in Downtown Boston on its release date. Even today I still love to picture Mom waiting in line and asking the staff there to find her a copy of the new 52's record for me.

"Butterbean!"

In the new wave-saturated 1980s, new album releases were like postcards from the future, and we studied every inch of the packaging to see what was coming. First, let's talk about album cover art: What gangly high school freshman didn't want to look like Simon Le Bon from Duran Duran back in 1985? How many girls got a Sinéad O'Connor haircut the minute they graduated from high school in 1987? Imagine going to prom in 1983 dressed even half as cool as David Bowie in his "Modern Love" suit and suspenders, or like INXS from the cover of their *The Swing* album? Long before Instagram, our "influencers" came to us through MTV and the pictures on the LPs and 45s and cassettes we endlessly thumbed through at our favorite record stores. That's how we learned to dress and groom like a proper punk/new wave/post-punk fan, and not just some suburban poser.

And the liner notes? Gen X set itself on a course for Lasik surgery thirty years later by obsessively squinting at the tiny-type credits and the mini-essays printed on each album (ostensibly written by the artists themselves). It was in those liner notes that we started to see that certain new wave singers, musicians, producers and engineers kept popping up all over the place on each other's records.

Like a "murder board" in a TV cop show with colorful strings showing how all the suspects are connected to the victim, '80s album liner notes revealed the existence of a rich musical conspiracy. Elvis Costello, Nick Lowe and Glenn Tilbrook from Squeeze seemed to be pals, singing backup vocals or playing guitar on each others' 1980s albums, time after time. Nick Lowe and Chrissy Hynde seemed to collaborate quite a bit. British record producer Hugh Padham had his audio fingerprints on several of our favorite records by the Police, XTC, the Human League and Split Enz. Joe Jackson played the fancy piano on Suzanne Vega's 1986 humble hit "Left of Center." Geoff Emerick, who was a young audio engineer working on the Beatles' *Revolver*, *Abbey Road* and *Sgt. Pepper's Lonely Hearts Club Band*, produced Elvis Costello's much-lauded Beatles-esque *Imperial Bedroom* in 1982. And Jerry Harrison, the multi-instrumentalist from Talking Heads, produced the Violent Femmes' third album, *The Blind Leading the Naked* (1986).

The more we studied the liner notes, the more we wanted to explore this vast musical ecosystem. But albums weren't exactly cheap for a teenage student in the mid 1980s. For inquisitive new wave fans on a tight budget, though, compilation and soundtrack albums were a gift from the musical gods. For $8.99 or so, a young wannabe punk/new waver could pick up albums like *Times Square* or the soundtrack to a little seen (in the U.S., at least) 1979 English film called *That Summer!*, which included hard-to-find tunes by the Boomtown Rats, Patti Smith, Elvis Costello, Ian Dury, Ramones, the Stranglers, Roxy Music and Richard Hell. Heck, that's better value than a McDonald's Happy Meal, which also debuted in 1979.

I never saw the 1983 film *Party Party*, but I treasure its soundtrack, which features obscure tracks by Sting, Midge Ure, Bananarama, Madness, Dave Edmunds and Elvis Costello. If you can get your hands on it, the 1987 CD sampler from Sire Records, *Just Say Yes*, is a post-punk 101 textbook: Depeche Mode's "Never Let Me Down," Echo &

the Bunnymen's "Lips Like Sugar," the Mighty Lemon Drops' "Out of Hand," and additional songs by Ramones, the Replacements, Aztec Camera, Throwing Muses, the Smiths and Erasure.

But wait! There's more! Don't forget to scour your favorite used record store for a copy of *Urgh! A Music War*, the 1982 double album that's stuffed to capacity with live performances by the Police, Wall of Voodoo, O.M.D., Oingo Boingo, XTC, the Go-Go's, Devo, Echo & the Bunnymen, X, Gang of Four and more. Many of the *Urgh!* performances can also be found on YouTube, and they are riveting.

And remember—before the new wave super-group Band Aid asked "Do They Know It's Christmas?" in 1984, other big-time fund-raising concerts yielded essential compilation albums that featured some classic new wave gems: *The Secret Policeman's Other Ball*, a 1981 benefit for Amnesty International, has Sting from the Police singing "Roxanne" and "Message in a Bottle" solo, and Bob Geldof from the Boomtown Rats doing an acoustic version of "I Don't Like Mondays;" and the 1981 album *Concerts for the People of Kampuchea* features live performances by the Pretenders ("The Wait," "Precious," "Tattooed Love Boys"), Elvis Costello and the Attractions, Rockpile (featuring Nick Lowe and Dave Edmunds), and a killer version of "Armagideon Time" by the Clash. I got a lot of mixtape mileage out of these compilations.

Another way Gen X stretched its meager vinyl budget was to trade in its used albums for cash or store credit at a used record store, like the one John Cusack owns in *High Fidelity*. You likely remember the drill: you'd buy a new album for $8.99 at the mall, you'd play it to death, populating endless mixtapes with tracks from it; you'd make a cassette copy of the whole album; and then you'd visit your favorite used record store, hoping to recoup a little bit of your original purchase price by trading it in. You'd hold your breath while the record store guy—it was always a guy—inspected your album for excessive wear and tear to determine its value; those fifteen seconds of used-album evaluation felt like an eternity, waiting for the record judge to pass a life or death sentence.

If memory serves you'd be lucky to get $2 in cash or $3 in store credit. Either way, you'd likely leave the store with just as many records as you came in with—sometimes more.

I really should have been saving my money for college, which I'd start in the fall of 1984. But as I grew more comfortable exploring the city I soon discovered that Boston had a used record store on every corner in the 1980s—the way there's a Dunkin' on every corner today.

By 1985 my little record collection was starting to catch up to my brother JB's.

ON YOUR RADIO

Hi, I'm Dave Grady, and it's, um, 3:06 on a Friday afternoon. Is there anybody out there? I mean, am I talking to myself? Are there people listening? And if so, where are you? And if so, who are you? And why don't you come down and tell me who you are, okay, and what you wanna hear and maybe I can play if for ya. Okay, see ya later.

IT'S MARCH 15, 1985, AND with high school mercifully behind me I'm a sophomore at Suffolk University on Beacon Hill in Boston. I'm spinning records in the WSFR ("Suffolk Free Radio") studio during the dreaded late Friday afternoon shift. The studio is almost the same size as the Devonshire newsstand that I still work at part-time (that is, it's pretty damned small), and the floor-to-ceiling shelves of vinyl albums make the place feel even smaller.

With no dorms for student housing quite yet, Suffolk in 1985 is still a "commuter school," meaning almost no one is on campus at 3:06 on the Friday before St. Patrick's Day in Boston. And without an FCC license, WSFR is only broadcasting in two buildings on campus—the student center and the cafeteria—via closed circuit.

I do not have millions of listeners. But I do have a handful of friends.

A whole bunch of us—Mike, Marc, and the other Mike we call "Mo," the other David, and Sue and Sandra and Connie and Lisa and Faith and Cindy and Kathleen and Doreen and Kevin and Cliff and Maureen and Liz and Rick and the rest—were classmates who quickly discovered that we had much in common: we all dreamed of careers in newspapers or radio or TV, and we all loved, loved, loved Depeche Mode, Tears for Fears, Echo & the Bunnymen and New Order.

Most of the members of our little new wave collective had a weekly one-hour show on WSFR, and we soon took control of the student newspaper, *The Suffolk Journal*, where we tended to write more album reviews than hard-hitting stories about the student government or tuition hikes. In 1986, I somehow finagled a press pass to a Q+A event at the Rat (again, Boston's modest but authentically filthy version of New York's CBGB club) to interview the Bangles.

The Bangles!

All the guys were ga-ga over Susannah Hoffs, and who could blame them, with that iconic side-eye she'd later perfect in the "Walk Like an Egyptian" video? Whoa. But to this day, I swear that bass player Michael Steele (who under the name "Micki Steele" was a founding member of Joan Jett's the Runaways back in the 1970s) gave me a very special look for at least one full second. Listening to Steele sing "Following" from their *Different Light* album still makes my tummy flutter. (Come to think of it, Michael Steele looked and dressed a lot like Steve Tyler from Aerosmith, with whom, as you may recall, I made a connection over some Beatles music and pornography at the Devonshire newsstand a few years earlier. But I digress.)

The *Suffolk Journal*, April 7, 1986

What was in rotation during my hour-long WSFR radio show that day in 1985? The surviving cassette tape tells the tale:

"Waterfront," Simple Minds.
"Lipstick Vogue," Elvis Costello.
"Gone Daddy Gone," Violent Femmes.
"Making Flippy Floppy," Talking Heads.
"I Confess," The English Beat.
"Prove My Love," Violent Femmes.
"Rough Boys," Pete Townsend
"All I Need Is Everything," Aztec Camera
"Messed Around," Squeeze.
"O My God," The Police.
"Head Over Heels," Tears for Fears.
"Let's Go To Bed," The Cure.

Not a lot of diversity there, I'll admit. No Romeo Void, Eurythmics, or Martha and the Muffins. No Lene Lovich, Eurogliders, Sinéad O'Connor, Siouxsie and the Banshees, Alison Moyet, or Aimee Mann. No Go-Go's, no Bangles, no Indigo Girls, and no Motels.

I'm sorry to say that I was not alone in this regrettable form of 1980s musical misogyny. When WFNX 101.7 FM, Boston's new wave radio station that we all adored, broadcast its "Top 101 Alternative Songs of the Decade" countdown on New Year's Eve 1989 (as voted by its listeners), only eleven of those 101 songs were by bands fronted by women.

(In addition to needing to get a little more expansive in what I was playing on my radio show, I also needed to get a lot less expansive in my Boston accent when I *talked* on the radio. My accent was early Matt Damon-esque insane back then, and you can listen to two minutes of me terrorizing the letter "R" on the air at WSFR at www.thosesongs.blog.)

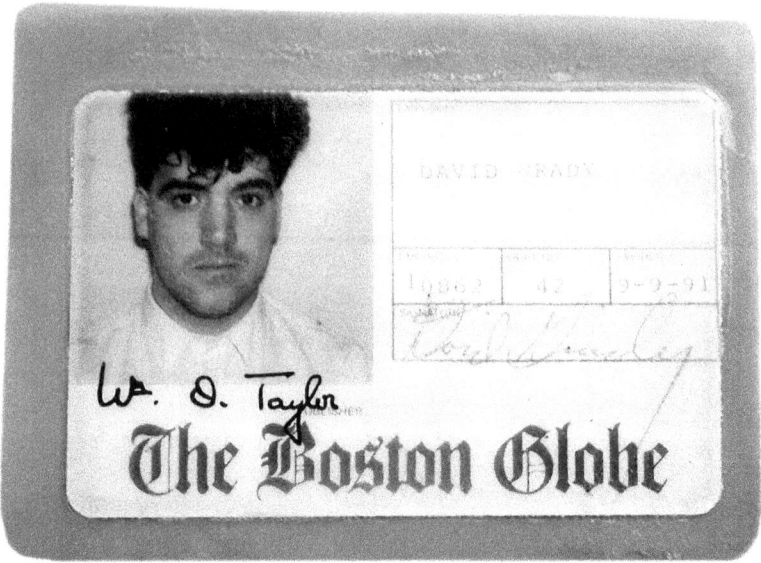

*When your wanna-be Robert Smith haircut
is too tall for your work ID.*

I LANDED AN INTERNSHIP at the *Boston Globe*, the biggest daily newspaper in New England, in 1987, and was lucky enough to write scores of articles over the next two years, even snagging a page-one byline after a plane crashed into a residential area in Boston's Dorchester neighborhood on my second night on the job.

I loved my time at the *Globe*, and I was particularly proud of the article I wrote about Boston's 1988 Gay Pride Day parade, which landed on page 46 of the Sunday paper on June 12. You have to remember that the cultural climate wasn't exactly gay-friendly back then (not that it's much better now): we were just a few years out from the shocking 1985 AIDS-related death of actor Rock Hudson; Ellen Degeneres wouldn't come out until 1997; same-sex marriage wasn't even legalized in the US until 2015. You probably had a few gay friends and a gay uncle or aunt (or two) in 1988 without even knowing it, and saying "drama fag" was still in style.

In my article about the Pride event, I made a point to call out the straight people on the parade sidelines who were showing their support and offering "free mom hugs" to the marchers. It was an upbeat article that captured the feeling of community on display, but I ended it with this:

> *Despite the air of celebration yesterday, the specter of AIDS hung over the festivities. Black balloons waved in the wind among the colorful ones carried by marchers, and a young man dressed as the Grim Reaper weaved in and out of line along the parade route. One man carried a sign that read "AIDS decided that some of my friends can't be here today."*

AIDS was a specter indeed, but I was just twenty-two when I wrote that article, naively believing I was far removed from the epidemic that would eventually take the lives of 42 million people worldwide. No, young and callow, I was more excited about having been allowed to review the Smiths' final album, *Strangeways Here We Come*, and Morrissey's debut solo album, *Viva Hate*, for the Thursday Arts section a few months earlier.

"This album makes depression fun," I wrote of *Viva Hate*.

Hmmm. Really?

The Smiths
STRANGEWAYS, HERE WE COME
Sire

Released just after the Smiths broke up last month, this album is the English quartet's most polished and diverse. Singer Morrissey again releases his loneliness and insecurity through alternately growling, lilting vocals. Yet even at his most morose, Morrissey can laugh while he cries. On "Unhappy Birthday," Morrissey's last wish before an imagined suicide is that his betraying lover gets sick from drinking too much. It's easy to find your foot tapping to "Girlfriend in a Coma," and even easier to dance along with "Death at One's Elbow," a rockabilly-flavored tune. Guitarist Johnny Marr counters Morrissey's downbeat lyrics with upbeat rhythms. Marr orchestrated the strings and reeds on several songs, adding both a tragic and playful backdrop. "Death of a Disco Dancer" is reminiscent of the Beatles' "Dear Prudence," complete with Lennonesque vocals and marching drumbeat. The Smiths saved their best album for last. — *David Grady*

Morrissey
VIVE HATE
Sire

Morrissey's first solo album is actually two albums. The former lead singer for the Smiths follows their tradition of painfully introspective ballads with wailing about unrequited love and loneliness. On the other hand the album signals a new and sometimes wierd direction for Morrissey. Guitarist and producer Stephen Street wrote the music, half the time capturing the old Smiths sound, the rest overindulging in wild guitar riffs and Beatle-esque string orchestrations. But Morrissey's lilting voice rises above the occasional musical calamity. "Suedehead" is wonderfully melodramatic, with Morrissey apologizing to a scorned lover, and "Everyday Is Like Sunday" is a haunting vocal tour-de-force. At seven minutes-plus, "Late Night, Maudlin Street" is an epic soul search that confirms Morrissey's position as king of pain. The album makes depression fun. — *David Grady*

WHO'S THAT GIRL?

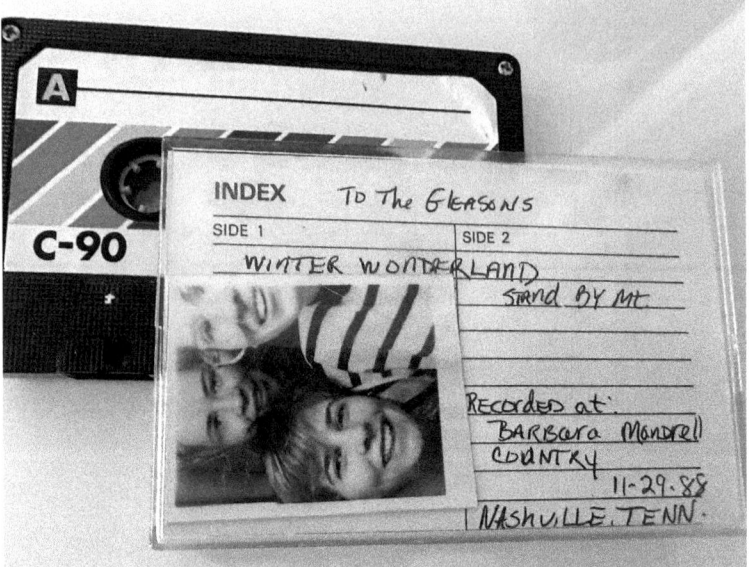

BY 1990 OUR FAMILY had moved out of the Devonshire, "us kids" now in our mid to late twenties, some poised to marry, most in serious relationships. We shared a sprawling "triple-decker" three-story rental house in a little town just north of Boston, and my brothers and sisters came and went as they pleased. That spring, I was unhappily winding down a relationship with a girl I'd met at Suffolk University in my seventh year there as an undergraduate student. (Two years as an intern at the *Boston Globe* had derailed my four-year plan to earn a degree.) No joke: D— looked a lot like Molly Ringwald, and she introduced me to the music of Tracy Chapman and the Sugar Cubes and that whole Lilith Fair roster, bringing some much-needed gender diversity to my future mixtapes. She was cool. I screwed it up, of course.

I found a job as a reporter for a small weekly newspaper—the *Brookline Citizen*—and became friendly with a graphic designer there named AJ. (AJ's boss, John M., played "Whole of the Moon" by the Waterboys on repeat on his boombox every Wednesday night when the whole staff would stay late to assemble the newspaper by pre-digital hand.)

AJ and I had vastly different tastes in music—he was a bit of a metalhead—but he surprised me one afternoon by suggesting we go to a concert at the Channel Club in South Boston; a band called

Concrete Blonde was playing that night, July 13, 1990, and their song "Joey" was a hit on the radio.

Famous locally for hosting some legendary hardcore punk rock shows over the years—Gang Green, Ramones, Jerry's Kids—the Channel Club had a reputation for being a pretty rough venue, and it was rumored that the Irish Mafia really owned the place. Back in the early 1980s, the cooler kids from my high school bragged about slam dancing at weekend afternoon All-Ages shows there, while I had never been bold enough to venture through the doors of that now-gone nightclub. But here we were in the brave new 1990s and I thought maybe it was time I tried. And anyway, I liked that Concrete Blonde song. "*Joey, baby, don't get crazy . . .*"

The floor was sticky and the place was packed. AJ disappeared to a far corner for a smoke (fourteen years before indoor smoking was banned in Massachusetts). Just then, a cute blonde girl caught my eye. I somehow found the courage to approach her, me wearing a long black John-Cusack-from-*Say Anything . . .* trench coat (despite the July heat), she wearing I don't remember what, but stand-out-in-the-crowd cute just the same. We stood next to each other, watching the show and exchanging a few shouted words between songs. Her name was Theresa.

The concert ended, and just as I leaned in to ask Theresa for her phone number (landline, of course: "do you have a pen?") an acquaintance from WSFR, the Suffolk University radio station, spotted me from across the dance floor and bolted towards me for a great big uninvited, unexpected hug.

Sloppy drunk, yet wildly high, Chris Somethingorother (not his real last name), was soooooooo happy to see me! Really! And he needed a ride somewhere, anywhere.

My new friend Theresa looked a little put off by the caliber of the intoxicated company I seemed to be keeping, but she gave me her number anyway, and I took Chris back to my apartment to let him sleep it off on the couch. On the ride home, AJ, my roommate, was not amused by the state of our guest.

Life imitates art, they say. There's a scene in that movie *Say Anything . . .* where John Cusack's character Lloyd Dobbler is on his first date with the girl he's obsessed with, Diane Court. They are at a wild high school graduation party. Diane looks a little put off when a sloppy-drunk-yet-wildly-high acquaintance of Lloyd's sees Lloyd and bolts toward him for a great big uninvited, unexpected hug. Lloyd confiscates his friend's car keys and helps him to the bathroom for a round of robust retching.

In the movie, Diane notes Lloyd's gentle empathy for his wasted friend, and she starts to fall in love with him. I like to think Theresa felt the same way about me when she saw me cart off my legless friend Chris for a ride home.

Did I mention John Cusack and I share a birthday?

Theresa and I convened a few days later at the European Restaurant in the North End for pizza and some non-shouting talking. I soon learned she was one of the youngest of eight kids (I may have mentioned herein once or twice that I'm the baby of seven), and that she'd been born and raised in Dorchester, the predominantly Irish-American Boston neighborhood where that airplane had crashed a few years earlier on my second night as a cub reporter at the *Boston Globe*. (Turned out Theresa's dad also worked at the *Globe*, in the basement helping compose the pre-digitized newspaper each night; he and I probably interacted hundreds of times during my tenure there. Boston's a small city.)

Dorchester is the kind of place (or it *was*, back in the '80s) where, when people ask where you live, you don't answer with a street name: you answer with the name of the closest Catholic church. (As in "I'm from St. Greg's, and this is my cousin Mikey from St. Mark's. We just went to that funeral at St. Brendan's.") Theresa had gone to Catholic schools for all twelve of her school years, while I was liturgical lightweight with just four years of parochial school under my belt. She was just starting her career in radiation therapy, treating cancer patients, and she loved the work. We both loved music. And eventually we loved each other.

Before we met, Theresa had been a far more adventurous music fan than I ever could be. In the 1980s, she and her friends had gone to see a bunch of cool bands play live at the Boston clubs that I was never brave enough to go to, like the Rat and the Metro in Kenmore Square. She'd already seen Hüsker Dü, Sinéad O'Connor and Midnight Oil live in concert, and her record collection was much more local, and much edgier, than mine. Theresa and her friends were chatty in an after-the-show "hey guys" way with bands like the Atlantics and the New Models. She knew a bunch of DJs from WBCN, the most popular FM rock station in Boston, and before I met her she had lived in London for a short time, where she and her friends were in the audience when the Fine Young Cannibals and the Jam performed their hits for a British TV show. (They loved the concert—and the free food set out for the young audience.)

A year or so older than me, Theresa was measurably cooler than I could ever hope to be. One night she showed me a picture of her first car, but all I could do was fixate on how much she looked like a Go-Go.

Theresa's new wheels 1981 Monte Carlo

Theresa had taken a road trip to Nashville in 1988 with some friends, and when she showed me the cassette tape from their recording session at a Nashville tourist trap, I knew she was the one. Here was a girl who also recognized the talismanic power of a cassette tape!

I gained a tiny bit of cool credibility with Theresa when we realized that we'd both attended the same General Public concert in 1989 at the Hynes Convention Center in Boston's Back Bay, less than a year before we met. We were probably just a few feet from each other, bopping on the dance floor to "Never You Done That" and "Tenderness."

That little concert hall is directly across the street from the building housing the public relations firm where, in 1999—ten years after that General Public show—I would help launch the recordable CD and drive a spike through the heart of the cassette tape industry.

Yes, that previous sentence just came out of nowhere, but I did in fact help kill off the audio format I truly loved.

Allow me to explain . . .

THAT TIME DICK CLARK AND I DECLARED WAR ON THE CASSETTE TAPE INDUSTRY

PHILIPS ELECTRONICS, THE FORTUNE 500 maker of big-screen televisions, MRI machines, electric razors and intelligent light bulbs, invented the modern audio cassette in 1963. In the summer of 1999, they hired me to kill the format.

Well, not *just* me. They also hired the Boston-based public relations agency where I happened to be working as a lowly copywriter. It would take a lot more people and talent than just this one thirty-three-year-old sweater vest-wearing guy to introduce a newfangled technology called "CD-R" to the masses—the recordable compact disc. And they hired Dick Clark—yes, *American Bandstand* Dick Clark—to help with the murder plot, too. (But more about his role later.)

In truth, killing off the cassette tape wasn't the overt goal of the worldwide PR campaign my co-workers and I spent night and day designing that summer in 1999. Now, more than twenty-five years later, I realize that the demise of the cassette mixtape was inevitable, no matter how well we did our job back then.

In the late 1980s and early 1990s, after decades of dominance by the vinyl record and cassette tape formats, the world of consumer music was all about the pre-recorded compact disc. Everyone wanted a Sony Walkman portable cassette player for Christmas when it launched in 1979, but when the Sony Discman launched in 1984 it quickly became a massive hit, too.

The 1982 debut of the CD format was a sonic game-changer: millions of long-haired music lovers, for example, first bought Pink

Floyd's *Dark Side of the Moon* on 8-track in 1973 for their car, and when the tape wore out (or when their Ford Pintos exploded), they sprung for the vinyl version in 1974. A few years later, they'd copy that vinyl onto a cassette tape as a gift for their 1980s college-bound siblings (who would soon be ignoring Nancy Reagan and saying "yes" to drugs while listening to "The Great Gig in the Sky"). And then, in the early 1990s, these OG faithful Floyd fans found themselves shelling out even more cash to buy *Dark Side of the Moon* once again, this time on CD.

By 1990, CDs were everything and everywhere. A Barbra Streisand CD carelessly dropped to the floor of a moving car was the key plot point in Albert Brooks's popular 1991 film *Defending Your Life*. An early e-commerce website, cdnow.com, launched in 1994—right around the time another little online startup called Amazon.com was just getting going. Amazon would soon add CDs to its online bookstore, slowly but surely killing off cdnow.

A Google search today reveals that close to 120 million CDs were sold in 1998 and 1999. By the summer of 1999 the pre-recorded cassette tape format was in late-stage hospice care, battered and beaten by the shiny compact disc to within 0.15-of-an-inch of its 60- or 90-minute life.

But for a certain population of hipsters, nerds, and music geeks, the allure of the cassette tape was undying. Discovering the mighty power of the "Pause" button on a cassette tape deck attached to a turntable was a critical rite of passage for many of us in the late 1970s and 1980s. Still, in early 1999 though, the idea of being able to record your favorite music onto a crystal-clear CD (like you could with a 99-cent blank cassette tape) seemed like something right out of the Jetsons.

Philips actually started making CD players that let music be "burned" onto a blank CD in 1997, but those machines were super-expensive—tools for professional audio engineers, not toys for your average home stereo owner. But with the year 2000 fast approaching, anything seemed possible—as long as we survived the Y2K bug. Plus, there was a creeping feeling that everything about music was changing further still.

Case in point: in June 1999, a very new thingy called Napster popped up on the fairly new thingy called the Internet, and, overnight, everyone was staying up way past their bedtime to smash and grab as many pirated MP3 music files as their 56K modems could handle. With Napster, you could amass a huge number of songs in digital format for free and then point and click and make a playlist of all your downloaded digitized songs. But for most people, their Napster- (or Kazaa, or LimeWire) acquired music was stuck on the hard drive of their Gateway 2000 desktop computers. Apple didn't even launch its iTunes store or the iPod until 2001.

And that's where Dick Clark, Mr. Rockin' New Year's Eve himself, comes in.

At the Boston PR firm, we'd come up with a great idea to help Philips Electronics publicize its new line of affordable recordable compact disc players designed for use in the home: we proposed an online contest, its rules and prizes to be loudly and repeatedly promoted on radio nationwide by Mr. Dick Clark in the waning weeks of 1999. The contest invited listeners to vote for the "Top 10 Songs of the Millennium" they wish they could easily put on to a blank CD—if only the equipment to do so existed.

Oh, but wait! Lucky for you listeners, Dick Clark explained over and over, Philips Electronics just happens to now make that very machine for the average consumer!

The contest results would be announced during *Dick Clark's New Year's Rockin' Eve* broadcast from Times Square on December 31, 1999. We called the PR campaign "the Millennium Mix Challenge," and I spent July and August of 1999 ghostwriting articles with titles like "The ABCs of CD-R" for paid-publication in audiophile magazines around the world. We were bringing music into the future and bringing the future of music into the home.

New Year's Eve 1999 finally arrived. The much-hyped Y2K bug failed to materialize, despite my anxious faith that society would crumble overnight and we'd all be living in a Mad Max-like hellscape in the morning. And the affordable, consumer-grade CD-R player was launched.

Are you surprised? Prince's "1999" topped the contest playlist and was voted the Number 1 song of the millennium. A bunch of lucky contestants won recordable CD players from Philips. The tech was the talk of the town, and a new era in audio had arrived. But, sick to death of all things CD-related after working on this product launch for months, I wasn't watching the Times Square New Year's Eve broadcast that night.

Instead, I was home alone, making my way through a pile of cassette tapes that I'd made exactly ten years ago to the very day.

As I mentioned earlier, on December 31, 1989, WFNX 101.7 FM— the wicked cool alternative radio station in Boston—did a "Top 101 Alternative Songs of the Decade" countdown, broadcasting live from all the cool but now long gone dance clubs, like Spit and Access. I went through at least six 90-minute tapes that New Year's Eve recording the broadcast, not wanting to miss a single track. Here's the list:

101. "Cat People (Putting Out Fire)," David Bowie
100. "Desire," Gene Loves Jezebel
99. "She Blinded Me with Science," Thomas Dolby
98. "Back on the Chain Gang," The Pretenders

97. "Rapture," Blondie
96. "Devil Inside," INXS
95. "The Ghost in You," The Psychedelic Furs
94. "Don't You (Forget About Me)," Simple Minds
93. "White Wedding," Billy Idol
92. "Birth, School, Work, Death," The Godfathers
91. "Beds Are Burning," Midnight Oil
90. "Abort," Tribe
89. "Need You Tonight," INXS
88. "Sledgehammer," Peter Gabriel
87. "Senses Working Overtime," XTC
86. "Lovesong," The Cure
85. "I Confess," The English Beat
84. "Under the Milky Way," The Church
83. "Gigantic," Pixies
82. "Lips Like Sugar," Echo & the Bunnymen
81. "Fascination Street," The Cure
80. "Two Hearts Beat as One," U2
79. "Suedehead," Morrissey
78. "Don't Change," INXS
77. "Just Can't Get Enough," Depeche Mode
76. "Infected," The The
75. "Bring on the Dancing Horses," Echo & the Bunnymen
74. "Clampdown," The Clash
73. "Cities in Dust," Siouxsie and the Banshees
72. "With or Without You," U2
71. "This Corrosion," The Sisters of Mercy
70. "The Killing Moon," Echo & the Bunnymen
69. "Private Idaho," The B-52's
68. "Precious," The Pretenders
67. "The Perfect Kiss," New Order
66. "More than This," Roxy Music
65. "Kingdom of Rain," The The (featuring Sinéad O'Connor)
64. "Red Rain," Peter Gabriel
63. "So Alive," Love and Rockets
62. "Bigmouth Strikes Again," The Smiths
61. "Lullaby," The Cure
60. "I Still Haven't Found What I'm Looking For," U2
59. "Closer to Fine," Indigo Girls
58. "Bittersweet," Hoodoo Gurus
57. "Avalon," Roxy Music
56. "Blood and Roses," The Smithereens
55. "That's When I Reach for My Revolver," Mission of Burma
54. "The Whole of the Moon," The Waterboys

53. "Rock the Casbah," The Clash
52. "Swamp Thing," Chameleons U.K.
51. "Slave to Love," Bryan Ferry
50. "Pretty Persuasion," R.E.M.
49. "The One Thing," INXS
48. "Mad World," Tears for Fears
47. "Alex Chilton," The Replacements
46. "Turning Japanese," The Vapors
45. "Why Can't I Be You?," The Cure
44. "Temptation," New Order
43. "E=MC2," Big Audio Dynamite
42. "Blister in the Sun," Violent Femmes
41. "Mayor of Simpleton," XTC
40. "Close to Me," The Cure
39. "Save It for Later," The English Beat
38. "Age of Consent," New Order
37. "With You," O Positive
36. "So. Central Rain (I'm sorry)," R.E.M.
35. "Pretty in Pink," The Psychedelic Furs
34. "Monkey Gone to Heaven," Pixies
33. "Let's Go to Bed," The Cure
32. "New Year's Day," U2
31. "Mandinka," Sinéad O'Connor
30. "(Every Day Is) Halloween," Ministry
29. "Fast Car," Tracy Chapman
28. "Fall on Me," R.E.M.
27. "A Night Like This," The Cure
26. "Birthday," The Sugarcubes
25. "Rise," Public Image Ltd.
24. "Inside Out," The Mighty Lemon Drops
23. "I Will Follow," U2
22. "Roam," The B-52's
21. "Running Up That Hill," Kate Bush
20. "Uncertain Smile," The The
19. "The Love Cats," The Cure
18. "Pride (In the Name of Love)," U2
17. "True Faith," New Order
16. "Burning Down the House," Talking Heads
15. "London Calling," The Clash
14. "In Your Eyes," Peter Gabriel
13. "Dear God," XTC
12. "Bad," U2
11. "Radio Free Europe," R.E.M.
10. "Blue Monday," New Order

9. "Once in a Lifetime," Talking Heads
8. "In Between Days," The Cure
7. "It's the End of the World as We Know It (And I Feel Fine)," R.E.M.
6. "Love Shack," The B-52's
5. "Sunday Bloody Sunday," U2
4. "She Sells Sanctuary," The Cult
3. "I Melt With You," Modern English (Nearly twenty years later, Modern English played a show in Boston, at the Paradise Club, on August 21, 2019, opening for the Alarm and the late, great Mike Peters. Theresa and I, of course, were there. There was a truly lovely moment when every single Boston-accented fan in the audience briefly adopted a broad English accent to sing along with "Melt With You." *Oi've seen the difference, and it's getting betta, aul the tyme.* Talk about "our music" providing a sense of community!)
2. "Just Like Heaven," The Cure
1. "How Soon is Now?," The Smiths

(Party game idea: Discuss and debate the merits of this list with your fellow Gen Xers and see who's the first to give up and go to bed.)

The act of recording this entire broadcast onto cassette on December 31, 1989 marked a turning point as meaningful to me as the Clash's arrival into our family home on December 25, 1980. The end of another era.

The minute the calendar turned to 1990 the music started to sound a little different: the Madchester Scene—with its fusion of dance music, rave culture and psychedelic rock—seemed to come out of nowhere and suddenly be everywhere. The Stone Roses and the Happy Mondays and the Soup Dragons were bringing a very different vibe compared to what many of us were used to from the Human League and Tears for Fears and U2. "Unbelievable" by EMF, with its aggressive sampling of comedian Andrew Dice Clay shouting "whaoooh!" landed like a gut-punch for a lot of Gen Xers whose musical vocabulary was built on a foundation of two bass guitar notes and simple plinking synthesizers. And Seattle grunge mania was just over the horizon, waiting to explode like a long-anticipated incoming nuke from Russia. The 1990s were here.

WFNX went off the air, traumatically for its faithful listeners, on July 20, 2012, its last song being the first one it had played when it launched on April 11, 1983: "Let's Go to Bed," by the Cure. The next day, the radio station was calling itself "The Bull, Boston's hit country station."

Yeehaw.

THOSE SONGS

IT'S LATE 1990, AND DESPITE having a wonderful time with my new girlfriend Theresa, I'm convinced I need to leave Massachusetts to find lasting work as a newspaper reporter. So I drive down to Florida alone to look for work while Theresa spends six weeks backpacking with a friend in Australia, as one does.

Before I put my stereo and my albums into storage, I kicked off my "Those Songs" project—making a series of 90-minute cassettes that would be my personal version of the WFNX "Top 101 Alternative Songs of the Decade" for my road trip.

The first mixtape in the series, *Those Songs Parts 1 and 2* (along with my beloved D-battery-powered Sanyo boombox) was stolen from my parked car on my first night in Florida. I really, really wish I could remember what was on that tape. It's my Lost Ark of the Musical Covenant, so if you ever see an old boombox with a tape inside called *Those Songs Parts 1 and 2* in a Florida thrift shop, please call me. There will be a substantial reward.

Those Songs Part 7 and 8 are also missing, and that one sometimes feels like an aching phantom limb. I suspect it had a fair amount the Church, Midnight Oil, the Alarm and the Smiths squeezed onto it.

But *Those Songs* Parts 3, 4, 5, 6, 9, 10, 11, 12, 13 and 14 survived the trip, and I still have them in a special shoe box, more than thirty-five years later.

I missed Theresa, but I had my mixtapes to keep me warm at night. Or, at least, most of them.

Florida didn't quite work out—I knew the day I left Boston that I'd be going back once Theresa returned from her walkabout Down Under anyway. I found a job writing press releases for the Mayor of Boston, Ray Flynn. Theresa and I got married in May, 1993. Predictably, we hired a WFNX DJ to spin alternative tunes at the reception, and our "meet the newly married couple walk-into-the-ballroom" song was "I'm On My Way" by the Proclaimers.

Crowded House's "Better Be Home Soon" was my mother-son dance.

It was a fun wedding, with a few hundred friends and family dancing the night away to '80s music. So many cousins, co-workers, old neighbors and new friends.

But my big brother JB wasn't there.

WHITE WEDDING
(WITH A LITTLE BLACK CLOUD)

JB DIED ON JUNE 19, 1992. It was the height of the AIDS epidemic, he was thirty-two years old and vulnerable, and that was that.

His full name was James Bernard Grady, Jr. In life, JB was a typical human—the kind of roommate who rarely washed out the sink after shaving and who ate all your Honeycomb cereal without asking. But in death and in memory, JB has become, for me, Steve McQueen cool and James Dean tragic: the first kid on the block to buy the new Clash album, the first in line for the new Jim Jarsmusch movie at the Nickelodeon Cinema, the first one in his gang of artsy friends to *really* rock a Members Only jacket.

Thanks to the mercies of selective memory, I now recall my big brother as the confident rock star who played a gig at a hipster bar in Cambridge, Massachusetts on February 13, 1984, and not as the annoyingly dedicated drumming student with whom I was forced to share a bedroom.

Thump, thump, thump, tap, tap, tap. High-hat. Cymbal Repeat. Ugh.

Still, despite the noise, I knew even then that my big brother was pretty damn cool. Sitting here now, more than three decades later, it occurs to me that my big brother has become less of a lost sibling to me and more like some kind of legendary celebrity I was lucky enough to have met several times when I was young and impressionable.

Like a star-struck fan feverishly scouring eBay, I've curated little pieces of memorabilia from our short time together: his album collection, of course; his Kodachrome slides filled with off-kilter images of 1980s Boston; the black and white Swatch watch he wore in the hospital that terrible, final week. These are among my most prized possessions.

As noted earlier, JB had started building one heck of a collection of punk/post-punk/new wave albums and 45s back in the early 1980s. Whenever he was out of the family apartment, studying Criminal Justice at Northeastern University in Boston or sneaking off to a concert at the Rat, I would carefully place one of his precious vinyl records onto his glittering Technics turntable.

My Aim is True, Elvis Costello.
London Calling, The Clash.
Entertainment!, Gang of Four.
Pretenders, The Pretenders.
Singles: 45's and Under, Squeeze.

I always made an effort to respect JB's records when I was making my mixtapes from his album collection, but I carelessly scratched the living shit out of his copy of Squeeze's *Singles: 45's and Under* one day, and I denied it forever. The guilt!

Some nights, pretending to sleep in the too-small-for three-brothers-so-we-had-a-trundle-bed bedroom (which very much smelled like teen spirit), I would watch and listen while JB crafted mixtapes for friends or lovers. He'd often take three hours to curate a 90-minute tape with the perfect balance of fast-slow-fast-slow songs, carefully choosing tracks from his LPs and his 45s to stitch together the perfect mix for some lucky recipient. And while he always muted the speakers and wore headphones to avoid incurring the wrath of Mom, I could still hear the music leaking out.

"Love My Way," Psychedelic Furs.
"New Toy," Lene Lovich.
"The Love Cats," The Cure.
"Never Say Never," Romeo Void.

You know—*those songs.*

JB got sick—I mean, really sick—in 1991, so of course I made him a mixtape. How else was I supposed to tell him how I felt? I mean, he was dying.

I called the tape *Harbor Towers, Volume 67,* named for the apartment building where our family had previously lived. Here's the playlist:

Side 1
"Cupid's Toy," Squeeze
"Four Seasons in One Day," Crowded House
"The Truth," Squeeze
"Memories Are Made of This," Dean Martin
"Pictures of You," The Cure
"Weather with You," Crowded House
"Obscurity Knocks," Trash Can Sinatras
"One Of The Best Ones," Bruce Cockburn (A brutal "goodbye song" with lyrics that include this humdinger: "*Guess I'd get along without you, if I had no choice, but please never make it so I have to . . .*")
"Fall on Me," R.E.M.

Side 2
"Old England," The Waterboys
"A Man is in Love, "The Waterboys
"Texarkana," R.E.M.
"Me In Honey," R.E.M. featuring Kate Pierson from the

B-52's.
"Without Love," Nick Lowe
"Just Like Heaven," The Cure
"Dream Attack," New Order
"A Life of Sundays," The Waterboys
"The Beat," Elvis Costello
"There is a Light That Never Goes Out," The Smiths
"When Ye Go Away," The Waterboys

That last song is a heartbreaker, with lyrics that include:

Your beauty is familiar
and your voice is like a key
That opens up my soul
And torches up a fire inside of me
Your coat is made of magic
and around your table angels play
And I will cry when ye go away

And that right there is the magical thing about mixtapes. They were the perfect mechanism for saying everything you couldn't say yourself—what the much-loved English band Squeeze called a "stereogram." You could make whatever flavor of mixtape you needed to make at that moment in life: the "sad breakup" tape, the "angry breakup" tape, the "I think you're cool and want you to think I am, too" tape.

The "you're dying and it's killing me" tape.

Art imitates life *and* death, I suppose. JB's last week in the New England Medical Center looked and felt very much like the last fifteen minutes of that 1993 movie *Philadelphia*, with family crowded around Tom Hanks's sickbed saying goodbye. It's extremely difficult for me, even thirty-three years later, to listen to that film's soundtrack without blubbering like a toddler who dropped his ice cream cone on the sidewalk. Still, it's a fantastic album, with tracks from Peter Garbiel, Indigo Girls and many others. Neil Young was nominated for Best Original Song for his song "Philadelphia," and Bruce Springsteen *won* the Oscar for his "Streets of Philadelphia."

(The film was directed by Jonathan Demme, who gave the world the gift of *Stop Making Sense*, the seminal 1984 Talking Heads concert film. Demme also directed the iconic music video for New Order's "The Perfect Kiss." But I digress.)

Gasping for breath in his hospital bed as the pneumocystis

pneumonia took hold, JB somehow managed to find the energy to politely ask the hippy-dippy hospital chaplain who had wandered into the room with a boombox playing "soothing" end-of-life New Age music, to "shut that shit off, please."

Knowing that a wake and a funeral were on the near horizon, I snuck out of JB's hospital room one afternoon to buy a suit at the Downtown Crossing Jordan Marsh department store. When I got back from my quick shopping spree, I bumped into Dad standing alone in the long, fluorescent-lit hospital hallway outside JB's room.

"He's gone," Dad said. He was a stoic guy, Dad was. But you could see the heartbreak in his tight eyes.

Like me and John Cusack, Dad and JB were birthday buddies. They shared April 2.

A week after JB's funeral, on my twenty-sixth birthday, Mom pulled me aside and discreetly handed me a birthday card. Tucked inside were two tickets to an upcoming U2 concert at Foxboro Stadium.

"I found these treasures in JB's room, and I know he would want you to enjoy them," Mom had written in the card. "This is his happy birthday to you."

JB was gone, but he was still giving me the gift of music.

FB0820 | 209 SECTION/AISLE | 7 ROW/BOX | 9 SEAT | ADULT ADMISSION
EVENT CODE
$ 30.00 RAIN/SHINE GATE4 30.00
PRICE
$
209 SECTION/AISLE
CA 163x ZOO TV —OUTSIDE BROADCAST
7 ROW/BOX | 9 SEAT — FOXBORO STADIUM
TPC598A THURSDAY EVENING
14MAY92 AUGUST 20, 1992 7:00PM

MTV PRESENTS
U2

PART 2

TIME, THE AVENGER

I WAS A BRILLIANT SURGEON back in the day, my eyes sharp, my hands steady. It didn't matter how mangled or twisted the mixtape was in the 1980s—I was the guy to fix it. I really knew how to twist a Number 2 pencil.

Fast forward forty years or so, and I've completely lost my touch. I recently performed my first emergency mixtape surgery in a *very* long time and it resulted in a very special patient dying on the table. *TransAtlantic Tunes/London Listening* was curated on a Maxell XLII-S 90 by my good friend Bob back in 1987. A gift for me perhaps, or maybe I stole it from the glove compartment of his battered 1974 VW Dasher. I like to think it was a gift.

Not too long ago, I popped Bob's thirty-eight-year-old tape into Deck A of my trusty (and apparently rusty) Technics Stereo Double Cassette Deck RS-T18. I made it through side A—"TransAtlantic Tunes"—and I greatly enjoyed what I heard:

"Echo Beach," Martha and the Muffins
"So Young," Elvis Costello
"Splitting into Three," Squeeze
"I Love the Sound of Breaking Glass," Nick Lowe
"Devil's Radio," George Harrison
"Paint by Number Heart," Martha and the Muffins
"Screw," The Cure
"Trust Me to Open My Mouth," Squeeze
"Tall Cool One," Robert Plant
"Simple Twist of Fate," Bob Dylan
"Women Around the World at Work," Martha and the Muffins

But when I pressed eject so I could listen to side B—"London Listening"—I noticed that the fragile magnetic tape had wound itself around the innards of the machine, looking like a bowl of black spaghetti. In 1987 I would have calmly declared a cassette "Code Red" and successfully implemented a complex series of life-support procedures. But here in 2023—older, out of practice, and ready for bed—I panicked.

My first mistake was using a pen, not a pencil. I untwisted that twisted tape as best as I could, but the more I worked on it, the worse it got.

I found my mini Phillips-head screwdriver in the kitchen junk drawer and boldly cracked that mixtape's sternum open, steeling my nerves for the life and death struggle ahead. I even asked Alexa to play some music to help me calm myself, and I'm not kidding (I'm not!) when I tell you "Doctor! Doctor!" by Thompson Twins came on.

"Alexa, stop!"

The X-rays and MRIs (fine—they're just pix I took with my iPhone) tell the story of the two futile hours that followed in the dining room OR.

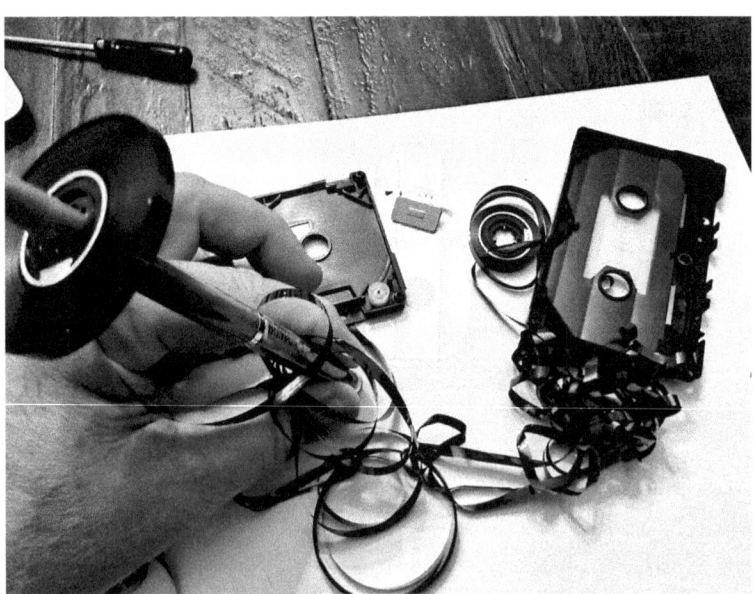

Time of death: 10:47 p.m. Sorry, Bob.

Accidents, as Elvis Costello reminds us, will happen.

A PRAYER FOR MEP

I LOVE A GOOD FLEA MARKET, where I always seem to come across some memory-jogging Gen X junk that makes me inordinately happy: political pins ("Nixon's The One!" and "McGovern, '72!"), old manual Royal typewriters, dog-eared *Life* Magazines, and rusty Hot Wheels cars abound. At a decent flea market you can always pick up a not-so-rare old-timey curiosity vinyl, like *Don Ho's Greatest Hits* or an off-label collection of classical music. And the fresh air is always welcome on a sunny Sunday Spring morning.

Flea market sellers typically scoop up big lots of old albums from estate sales, which is why I see three or four copies of the *South Pacific* soundtrack (1958) or *The Greatest Vocalists of the Big Band Era* in the used record bins *every* time I go to my local flea market. The older generation is steadily dying off, and their once-prized albums have no one left to love them, so they end up in a $2-per-album stack next to a pile of vintage *TV Guides*.

A few years ago I spent just $1 on a scratchy copy of the Moody Blues' *Days of Future Passed* (1967, featuring "Nights in White Satin") at my local flea market, noting the words "This Album Belongs To MEP" written in faded blue ink on the back. As I handed over my cash, I silently said a prayer for MEP, whom I assumed had been the dearly-departed cause of a recent nearby estate sale.

When my neighborhood flea market opened this year after its long winter break I couldn't help but stop by to check out the latest batch of estate sale finds. I really shouldn't be spending money on used albums—I have more than enough records already and the house needs a new roof and there's that retirement fund over there crying for attention—but it's hard to resist. This time, though, I came across a disturbing number of classic alternative records sharing space with the old Bing Crosby records.

On a recent Sunday, I found *Synchronicity* by the Police (1983), the *Pretty in Pink* soundtrack (1986), and singles by O.M.D., Devo, and the Eurythmics. The following Sunday, I found a pile of used cassette tapes that included *Get the Knack* by the Knack (1979), and *Whammy!* by the B-52's. I couldn't imagine a living soul who would willingly give up these records and tapes.

And then it hit me: they aren't, and they didn't.

I decided right then and there to skip the flea market for the foreseeable future and instead spend my Sunday mornings at home listening to the records I already own.

Before it's too late.

GOODBYE GIRL

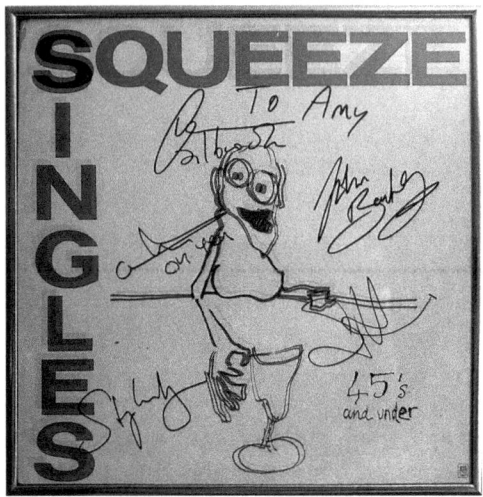

IN *HIGH FIDELITY*, THE 2000 FILM starring my birthday buddy John Cusack, we learn that Mr. Cusack's character Rob Gordon has almost 1,500 albums in his personal collection. From the perspective of some people, that's insane. But for many of us it's an enviable and aspirational figure.

Me? I love my records, but I'm not one of those hardcore audiophiles who search the internet far and wide for rare limited-edition Japanese mono versions of their favorite albums—not that there's anything wrong with that level of new wave devotion. And I'm just not the type to spend thousands of dollars on high-end analog audio components, either; somehow I've managed to keep my brother JB's Technics turntable in working condition for thirty plus years. Also, I have nothing against CDs, Sirius Radio, Pandora, "smart speakers," or MP3 players with cheap wired headphones. I have 339 LPs, 155 of which are very much *not* in the classic alternative family. I also have 174 singles, of which only 45 are *no*t new wave, punk, or punk-adjacent. There are 463 CDs crammed into a bookcase in my basement family room, 3,894 songs (combined) on the last two functioning iPod Shuffles in my house, and 11,048 MP3s trapped in iTunes on my too-risky-to-connect-to-the-internet 2007 Windows Vista laptop.

And I absolutely hate that my record collection grew by three in 2023, when my good friend Amy passed away at the ridiculously young age of fifty-six.

A girlfriend for a minute in the late '80s and a lifelong friend thereafter, Amy was the epitome of '80s cool. She wore leather penny loafers with actual pennies in the slots on top, pegged Guess blue jeans, crisp white button-down shirts, and a wicked cool leather jacket. Her jet-black bobbed haircut always made me think of the hyper-nerdy, adorable character Jordan from the Val Kilmer 1985 cult classic *True Genius*. Amy wasn't just a fan of certain new wave bands: she was a staunch advocate, forever reminding her ever-widening circle of friends about the brilliance of Adam Ant, the English Beat, the Selecter, and the Specials. She had all the 2-Tone band T-shirts. She had all the band buttons. Her collection of 1980s concert tickets deserves its own wing at the Punk Rock Museum in Las Vegas.

At some point in the early 2000s, Amy landed a job at a company that operated comedy clubs and movie theaters and live music venues all across the Boston area. One night, she got me and Theresa into the "Showcase Live" concert hall in Foxboro, Massachusetts, to see Squeeze play a show. The band did a "meet and greet" right after their performance, but Theresa and I had to get home to pay the babysitter, so we missed out. Amy stayed and got her copy of Squeeze's *Singles: 45's and Under* signed by every member of the band. *Jealous!*

In the mid-2010s Amy developed a ruthless and hateful neurological condition, putting many of her passions—attending Boston Red Sox games at Fenway Park and going to concerts—painfully out of reach. Like my brother JB years before, she grew smaller and smaller over time.

On June 15, 2019, Theresa and I took Amy to Boston's House of Blues to see the Specials in concert, lugging her wheelchair to the door and escorting her to a special reserved seat in the first row. That was a good show, and a great night for all three of us.

Before she got sick, Amy would often visit me and Theresa and our three children at our home, bringing cartons and cartons of delicious homemade ice cream. It was a burgeoning hobby, and she was good at it. My kids, especially my youngest Ethan, adored her. They both had the tiniest hint of a lisp, so they were simpatico that way. Thimpatico, I suppose.

Amy was a devout Christian, and she never lost her grace (or her Pee-wee Herman-inspired sense of humor) when she got sick. But she knew the score. A few weeks before she passed, Amy and I spent an afternoon together with her mom Joy, and her sister Sue. At her childhood home's kitchen table, with my help, Amy fired up an old laptop and slowly navigated to an outdated version of iTunes. She hit "play" on a song she wanted me to enjoy with her. It was "Perfect Day," by Lou Reed (1972), a haunting ballad (produced by David Bowie) that radiates sadness, joy, hope and resignation—all at once.

At her memorial service a few weeks later I learned that Amy had repeated this musical ritual with many of the old friends who had come calling, knowing that her time was running out. What a gift to each and every one of us! In her eulogy, Amy's twenty-something niece mentioned the many mixtapes that Amy had gifted her over the years, calling her "the cool aunt." More than a few people attending the church service were wearing the band buttons she had gifted them in recent weeks during their pilgrimages to see her before her departure.

The afternoon of my visit, that "perfect day" a few weeks earlier as I said goodbye for what I knew would be the last time, Amy told me she had a special present for me. Two 45s: "Everybody's Happy Nowadays / Why Can't I Touch It" by the Buzzcocks (1979), and the Cure's "Hot Hot Hot !!!", backed by "Hey You !!!" (1987). Amy and I used to go used record shopping together in Boston's Kenmore Square, back around 1987 or so, drawn to the eclectic and affordable collection of used vinyl at Planet Records. I suspect she may have purchased those 45s on one of our nights out, before we grabbed a slice at the Pizza Pad next door.

A few weeks after the memorial service, Amy's sister Sue gifted me Amy's framed and autographed copy of *Singles: 45's and Under*—a pristine copy of the same record that I had once borrowed from my brother JB and ruined with a deep and ugly scratch.

Amy's last gift to me hangs prominently on the wall of my home office, next to a quote from a hymn we sang at her service ("Great is Thy Faithfulness") that I printed out in 32-point type:

Strength for today
And bright hope for tomorrow.

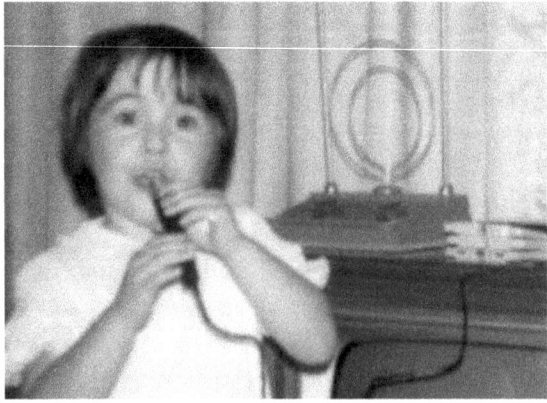

Amy, 5, already making cassettes.

YOU'VE GOT MAIL

NOT TOO LONG AGO I OPENED my mailbox to find a small package sent by my big brother Eddie, the Bob Seger fan, who now lives in Florida.

Inside the padded envelope was a cassette tape.

DRUMROLL, PLEASE

IT'S NOT QUITE A DRUM SOLO FOR the ages, but the first few beats of the Pretenders' 1983 radio hit "Middle of the Road" *are* pretty cool. And if you're of a certain age, it's likely you can close your eyes and play that staccato drum riff in your head, clear as an FM-radio signal.

Bah, bah babba baba ba
badda da dum
batta dum
batta dum dum
dum
dum dum dum dum dum dum
bam—cymbal crash!

And those lyrics about the bloody third world where the babies just come with the scenery! Fun song. I gotta tell you though: that opening drum riff sounds much better to my ears when my brother JB played it. JB and his classmates were students at the John Payne School of Music in Boston—an early *School of Rock*-type outfit without the Jack Black—and their final exam was to play a show at the old Ryles Jazz Club in Cambridge, Massachusetts. It was February 13, 1984, and they started their set with "Middle of the Road."

I was in the audience for that "intimate" concert, a seventeen-year-old sipping warm soda in a cold bar with my parents and a few of my other siblings, cheering on this raggedy little rock ensemble. And someone—maybe me?—hit "record" on the boombox that had been placed way too close to an amp.

This was the tape my brother Eddie sent me in the mail forty years later.

The concert was fun. The "Rock Ensemble" was, um, a little rough around the edges, but their set was joyous just the same. All those months sharing a bedroom with my brother the drum student suddenly felt worth it. And now, whenever "Middle of the Road" comes on the radio, I think of that concert and I picture my big brother up there on stage, twenty-three-years-old that night, healthy and cooler than cool, almost keeping time on the drum kit.

JB on the drums.

Like many of us on the spectrum of always-on musical fandom, I recently bought one of those gadgets that lets you digitize your old cassette tapes. (It all comes around, full circle, doesn't it?) So you can actually listen to my brother and the Rock Ensemble playing at www.thosesongs.blog.

And when you're done listening, ask yourself: which version do you like better? The Pretenders' version? Or JB and the Rock Ensemble's take on the song?

Now come on, baby!

You know which one I think is best.

I put the cassette tape in my special shoebox (Converse All Stars, of course) that holds two dozen or so other audio telegrams from the past, including a 90-minute mixtape that's missing about 90 per cent of its label. Just one listen to this mystery tape tells me that JB made it sometime in the early 1980s for himself or a friend—although I like to think he made it especially for me. The playlist perfectly captures my big brother's transition from a 1970s suburban classic rock kid to a clean-cut 1980s punk. What's on it?

Side 1

"Town Without Pity," Ronnie Montrose

"Jump," Aztec Camera

"A Day Without Me," U2

"The Thrill of It All," Roxy Music

"1984," David Bowie

"Heaven (Must Be There)," Eurogliders

"I Would Die 4 U," Prince

"We Live as We Dream, Alone," Gang of Four

"Friends," The Police

"Reelin' in the Years," Steely Dan

"All I Need is Everything," Aztec Camera

"(Don't Go Back To) Rockville," R.E.M.

Side 2

"New Frontier," Donald Fagan

"The Music Never Stopped," Grateful Dead

"Woody and Dutch on the Slow Train to Peking," Rickie Lee Jones

"Average Person," Paul McCartney

"Alice's House," Psychedelic Furs

"Please Please Please Let Me Get What I Want," The Smiths

"Misfits," The Kinks

"Up on the Catwalk," Simple Minds

"Knockin' on Heaven's Door (live)," Eric Clapton

"For You Blue," The Beatles

I put this particular mixtape on every now and then, usually in April on JB's birthday or on the cursed day of June 19 to mark his passing.

I listen, I sing along, and I try to think good thoughts.

BIG QUESTIONS

SOMETIMES I SIT AND look at that tape-filled Converse shoebox and I wonder: should I stop playing these precious, aging artifacts so much? Should I hide them under the bed to keep them safe from the risk of further age-related injury? Or should I play them whenever the manic musical mood strikes—audio death and dismemberment be damned? And then I wonder further: am *I* getting too old to be dancing around the kitchen to this music, as well? Maybe I should put on a nice work-related podcast and act my age.

Intrusive thoughts like these make me realize that, on behalf of all of Generation X, I need professional help. And by "professional help," I mean conversations with record store owners, DJs, musicians, and maybe even a world-renowned expert or two in the psychology of music. These are the people who likely feel and think about '80s music the same way I do, the same way *we* do; I'm hopeful they can offer some helpful perspective on the following Big Gen X Life Questions:

- Should we feel "really old" or "young-at-heart" when we hear a New Order song playing over the PA system in a hotel lobby or at the dentist?

- Do "our songs" make us happy when we're feeling sad, or do those songs (and the persistent memories they carry) make us sad when we're happy?

- Is nostalgia a warm, comfortable blanket that offers us shelter from a hostile and overwhelming world? Or is it the cold kitchen floor we slipped on while dancing to "The Safety Dance?"

  Let's find out.

IT'S NOT THE YEARS,
IT'S THE MILEAGE

Bruce the Bear

FIRST, I START TO TACKLE the "age thing" by trying to get in touch with Larry the Duck, a DJ on the SiriusXM satellite radio channel First Wave.

Larry the Duck has been spinning classic alternative music professionally since "our music" was new in 1979, so I figure he's got to be around sixty-seven years old. These days, in addition to dropping names of the many new wave artists he's met over the years, Mr. the Duck hosts a seven-day "'80s Cruise" on the Royal Caribbean cruise line—an event that, via social media posts, looks both compelling and repellent. Sure, '80s nostalgia is Larry the Duck's livelihood, but my goal is to get his perspective on why he thinks his many fans stay glued to his '80s music station when there are 150 or so other channels to choose from on SiriusXM.

Do people tell him that his playlists make them feel young, or happy, or something else?

But Larry the Duck doesn't respond to my polite email request for a little chat, so I happily settle for Bruce the Bear, who, for the record, does not feel too old to enjoy new wave music.

At sixty-seven years old, Bruce the Bear is a DJ at WKKL-FM, the student radio station at Cape Cod Community College in Barnstable, Massachusetts that only plays late '70s and 1980s new wave music. I've been listening to WKKL for a few years (and you can, too, by asking your "smart device" to "stream WKKL on Tune-In"). Since 99 per cent of the other DJs are clearly students in their late teens and early twenties, I figured Bruce must be the station's program manager, or maybe a teacher at the school. Turns out he's an undergraduate student, just like the rest of them, working on his degree.

"People told me, for decades, that I had a face for radio, so I decided I was going to do something with it," Mr. the Bear tells me. "I came here to study broadcasting, and I'll tell you—I *know* I have a *voice* for radio. I enjoy the hell out of it. I'm on air three times a week, Wednesday nights from 5:00 to 7:00, Friday mornings from 8:00 to 10:00 a.m., and Saturday night from 5:00 to 6.00. I'm Bruce the Bear, and my loyal listeners are known as my 'Bear Cubs.' When this semester is over I'll get around to getting bumper stickers printed up that say 'I'm a Bear Cub: Listen to Bruce the Bear on 90.7 FM.'"

Sitting on a rickety picnic bench outside the WKKL studio—two double-wide trailers stitched together on the outskirts of campus—Bruce the Bear smiles broadly as he recalls living in Georgia in the 1980s. "I always loved Bob Marley, the Cranberries, the B-52's, Talking Heads especially," he tells me. "The people who lived across the street from me in Atlanta used to have B-52's raves, and Talking Heads raves, so you couldn't sleep. You just had to go over and dance."

When he's not in class or on the air, Bruce works the parking lot at a Trader Joe's grocery store on Cape Cod, retrieving errant grocery carts. "When I say 'hello,' people know my voice!"

Clearly, new wave music is honey to Bruce the Bear. Since almost all of his fellow college DJs are hardly past the legal drinking age, I ask him what it's like to be the only adult in the room.

"I'm sixty-seven," he says, "but I'm far from an adult."

SHOWTIME

```
GW0805  1  SECTION 20X  J  25      ADULT
  17.50  RAIN OR SHINE        17.50
PRICE & ALL TAXES INCL
  CC1.85  WBZ TV 4 AND MILLER MUSIC
    1
    1  SECTION BOX
 CA    5X  NO CAMERAS/TAPE/BEVERAGES
    T  25      THE SMITHS
   ROW   SEAT
OHM1202     $1 PARKING INCILUDED
A 4AUG6   TUE AUG 5, 1986 7:30PM
```

TALK TO A PERSON WHO is not a semi-obsessive classic alternative music fan and they'll seem genuinely surprised that anyone would want to see an '80s band live in concert more than a few times, especially decades after those bands topped the charts.

When I tell new friends and acquaintances that I've seen Squeeze in concert at least twenty times (and Elvis Costello fifty-two times over the last forty years or so), they shake their heads in disbelief, saying something like "that's crazy." But when I point out that they've probably gone to forty or more Red Sox games in their lifetimes—the Sox play eighty or so home games each year, for goodness' sakes—they just don't see the two experiences as the same. They're proud to put their Fenway Park selfies on social media, but they're scandalized when *you* post your snapshot from a Tuesday night Gang of Four concert at the Paradise Club, just a mile or two up the street from the ballpark.

It seems that some people view new wave concert-going after a certain age as a sign of arrested development.

And then there are people like Kristen B., who know for certain that concert-going is good for the aging soul.

In April 2025, Kritsen celebrated her sixtieth birthday with a half-dozen friends by attending a B-52's concert at the Venetian hotel and casino on the Las Vegas Strip. Dressed like retro go-go girls in colorful mini-dresses, knee-high white leather boots and faux beehive hairdos, the seven friends had travelled—no joke—from Idaho to hear the B-52's sing "Private Idaho" and fourteen other career classics that night. Theresa and I were there, too.

I introduce myself to Kristen B. and her friends in the theater lobby before the show, theatrically waving to my wife to join us so these nice ladies won't think I'm trying to get any of them back to *my* love shack. I ask Kristen if concerts like this make her and her friends feel young or old.

"Young," she replies, without hesitation and with obvious glee. "The thing is, we all love to dance and we really want to go see the Go-Go's next! I dressed like one of the Go-Go's for Halloween back in 1982, and I looked really cute! This is what I grew up with and . . . now my three kids know all of this music." Theresa tells Kristen that our three kids were raised on those songs, too, and asks how old her children are. They're twenty-three, twenty-six and twenty-nine, Kristen says—exactly the same ages as our kids, of course.

Me, making new friends at the B-52's show in Vegas.

Next, I intrude upon Scott and Ziggy, a couple in their early and mid sixties who have also traveled from afar to see the B-52's. College-age sweethearts who went their own ways more than thirty-five years ago, Scott and Ziggy reconnected after their respective divorces and are positively adorable together today. Ziggy is wearing a flowing gold lame gown, and Scott is dressed like Joe Jackson circa 1981, complete with the black bowler hat. They tell me they lived in different states when they first got back together and would meet in the middle at a place they called—yup, you guessed it—their love shack. Concerts like this one *always* make them feel young, they told me.

(At one point in our quick conversation, Scott asks me to find the video for Fleetwood Mac's 1979 song "Tusk," on my smartphone. You may remember that song featured a mesmerizing drumbeat and the rousing music of the USC marching band. I find the video, and Scott tells me to pause at the thirteen-second mark. Yup, that's him, playing the trombone.)

The show will start soon, so I quickly introduce myself to a fifty-ish looking couple, Chris and Lisa, who flew in for the concert from North Carolina. Lisa is sporting a pair of bright red lobster earrings. "The B-52's were my first concert without my parents, back when I was thirteen," she tells me. The show was at the Carowinds, a popular amusement park on the North/South Carolina border. "I went with three or four friends, and we're lifelong B-52's fans now."

Husband Chris chimes in: "I remember when my older sister brought their first album home back in the seventies!"

The house lights blink a few times, a five minute warning for showtime. "I love it, because it reminds me of being so young and fun," Lisa says as she pushes back from the lobby bar to find her seat inside the theater. "Like, I can't wait for the show to start."

Theresa and I find our seats. Onstage, singers Kate Pierson, (at showtime, just a few weeks shy of her seventy-seventh birthday), Fred Schneider (seventy-two, and rocking a pair black Converse Chuck Taylors) and Cindy Wilson (sixty-seven, and still a hell of vocalist and bongo player) radiate pure energy and joy, from start to finish. Kate and Cindy belt out the harmonic high notes and dance non-stop with apparent ease for nearly eighty minutes. Between songs, Fred charms the audience with little jokes and stories delivered in his iconic Planet Clare-meets-Athens, GA accent. About thirty minutes into the show, the 1,800 or so graying Gen Xers pogo dancing in their seats seem a lot more winded than Fred, Kate or Cindy. I can see Scott and Ziggy down in front, dancing like nobody's watching.

On a big screen behind the very tight backup band, random clips from three decades of B-52's music videos play, occasionally spotlighting Cindy's handsome brother Ricky, the band's outrageously talented guitarist who died in 1985 from complications related to AIDS. He was thirty-two, just like my brother JB.

In its review of the show, the *Las Vegas Sun* wrote: "But for the famous three-word line in 'Love Shack,' 'Tin roof, rusted!' there was no rust on this show, just a night of songs that transported us back."

Going to live concerts provides yet another effective method of tuneful time travel: T-shirt-watching, which is a more polite and interesting version of people-watching. Theresa and I recently saw Simple Minds play at the old "Great Woods" amphitheater just south of Boston, with opening acts Modern English and Soft Cell, and the line for the restrooms looked like the catwalk at a classic alternative fashion show. Vintage Tears for Fears T-shirts. Violent Femmes.

More than a few English Beat tees, with those iconic black and white 2-Tone characters on scooters and wearing skinny ties and mini-skirts. Joy Division T-shirts, of course, and plenty of Duran Duran, the Specials, Squeeze, Midnight Oil and Depeche Mode shirts. I was reminded of the many concert shirts that I overpaid for at merch tables over the years, and I decided right then and there to be *happy* with the memory of owning them in the first place, rather than being sad about the loss of those cool shirts (and my waistline) over time.

My favorite T-shirt at that Simple Minds concert, though, was worn by a woman who appeared to be in her late sixties, which read (in neon-colored lettering) "Powered by 80s Music!" I tried to introduce myself as she passed, but she walked too fast for me and disappeared into the gray-haired crowd before I could catch up.

On stage, Modern English frontman Robbie Grey urged the audience to get on its feet. "Stand up," he shouted with a showman's smile. "You're not dead yet!"

FOREVER YOUNG

I VIVIDLY RECALL A HUMID summer night years and years ago—1999 or 2000 maybe—when I went to a Squeeze concert at the waterfront Pavillion in Boston and noticed the fragile gentleman ahead of me in the beer line using one of those metal walkers that had tennis balls for feet. I remember feeling conflicted: *that'll never be me*, I thought, even though my own legs kinda hurt at the time. Didn't the German synth band Alphaville tell us we'd be "Forever Young" in 1984? For Gen X, hearing the music of our formative years today can make us feel like sad dinosaurs, or it can make us feel young and happy. The choice is ours.

For some of us, as we grasp and reach for a youthful leg of hope, it's not enough to just play the air guitar when a Violent Femmes song comes on the radio. Age and propriety be damned, many of us feel a burning need to join the new wave bands we love so much, if only for just a few minutes. "Looking for a good song I can sing at a new wave karaoke night coming up," read a recent post on the "80s New Wave" page on Facebook. "Female vocalist preferred and that's the problem, all my faves are usually sung by men. All suggestions welcome!" Within minutes, more than 200 Gen Xers had chimed in with suggestions ranging from Cindi Lauper and Yaz to Missing Persons and Kate Bush. (Me? My shameless go-to karaoke song is Nick Lowe's "Cruel to be Kind," and the audience usually chooses kindness over cruelty when I take to the mic . . . not because I'm any good, but because karaoke people tend to be nice and often view karaoke as a form of helpful group therapy.)

I was never one for the air *guitar*—that privacy-of-your-own-home version of instrumental karaoke that makes the kids cringe but makes people our age feel cool for a minute or two. But in my dreaming head and my empty hands I've been an accomplished air-*bassist* since at least 1985. Theresa and our three kids seemed to have taken notice, and back in 2016 for my fiftieth birthday they presented me with a shiny new Fender four-string P-bass and an amp. It was a not-so-subtle suggestion that it was time I put up or shut up about the awe I experience whenever I hear the bass being played by Graham Maby from Joe Jackson's band, Tina Weymouth from Talking Heads, or Peter Hook from Joy Division/New Order.

I can be very annoying doing that verbal and ridiculous-finger-movement "boom boom doop" air-bass thing when the right song comes on.

A real live bass guitar was a terrific fiftieth birthday present, honestly. So thoughtful. The thing about playing a bass, though, is that you actually have to know how to play the bass.

Sure, Sid Vicious couldn't play a note, and he got away with it. And while I didn't know Sid Vicious, I do know that I am no Sid Vicious. I took a few lessons with a very patient instructor at the local music school who tried to teach me the bassline to "Middle of the Road," and I loved the fact that the four strings on the bass were for the E, A, D and G notes: **E**van **A**nd **D**avid **G**rady—Evan being my first-born, at this point a skilled self-taught guitarist himself.

I practiced—a little—but it became apparent pretty quickly that I had neither the attention span nor the discipline required to justify the time and expense of proper lessons. Old dog, new tricks and all that. Woof.

Still, I didn't hide the guitar (or my shame) in a closet, and I didn't pretend that I didn't want to play bass like a Pretender after all. Instead, I adopted the same strategy I used in my high school keyboarding classes between Franciscan Friar beatings: use four fingers and forget the rest. In 1982, I taught myself how to type fifty words per minute with just two index fingers and two thumbs. In 2016, that's exactly how I played the bass in my little basement man-cave. (It's also how I typed this book in 2025.)

Four fingers across two hands are just enough to play the bass along with a handful of punk/new wave songs and feel like you know what you're doing without having any actual talent. With just four fingers, I mastered the extraordinarily complex (kidding!) spinal bass lines of Gang of Four's "Damaged Goods," the Cure's "A Forest," and even "Mystery Achievement" by the Pretenders. Who knows? Maybe I'll pick the damned thing up again soon, and with some more practice I might even learn how to play along to "Psycho Killer."

In short, I'm an amateurish amateur. But then there are the people who rise far above "wannabe karaoke star" status and take their love of '80s music to a whole new level. So, please let me introduce you to Petra DeLuca and Dan Powell, members of a popular '80s new wave cover band Melt With You, who can actually play their instruments and sing—and who have developed quite a fan base throughout and across Pennsylvania.

The six-piece band plays faithful covers of strictly '80s new wave music—plenty of Blondie, the Cure and the Clash—but no Journey, no Billy Joel, no Van Halen covers. Their "regular" shows are dance parties with all the '80s flair: ninety-nine red balloons will in fact float around the dance floor when the band sings that Nene Hagen hit from 1983. Two or three times a year, the band throws an "80's prom" or "homecoming" event, complete with the crowning of the king and queen of the prom.

"We do happy," says Petra, the band's vocalist. "We make people feel good. That's important."

"People who love this stuff love this . . . and it sort of defines their personality," adds Dan, the band's rhythm guitarist. "It's like, they feel seen and feel like they're part of a community."

Petra is fifty-two years old, and she's been knee-deep in Gen X new wave music for quite some time. "I grew up in Europe and was obsessed with Duran Duran when I was in about eighth grade, and then I became obsessed with A-ha, then I became obsessed with Boy George," she tells me on a recent Zoom call. New wave music was omnipresent in Europe during her formative years, she says. "There was a huge saturation of new wave. It wasn't really compartmentalized, it was just everywhere and we all loved it . . . and you know, give me a guy in eyeliner any day, I'll be happy."

"People come up at the end of a show brimming with requests," adds Dan, fifty-eight. "Do you play 'Safety Dance'? Can you play this? Could you play that . . . ? We're like crack dealers—the first song is free, and they love it, and they come back and bring their friends."

The average age of attendees at a Melt With You concert is around forty-five—the precise Gen X cutoff point, for those who take their generational striation seriously—but both Petra and Dan mention the pleasantly surprising number of younger people at their recent shows: "The latest show, there was a bunch of twenty-two-year-olds up front," Dan tells me. "Many of them grew up with all these songs in their house from their childhood."

Adds Petra: "Some of these kids know more songs from Siouxsie and the Banshees than I do."

Our songs have become family heirlooms—musical artifacts that bring generations together, like campfire stories told to a backbeat of drum machines and synthesizers.

TALKIN' 'BOUT
MY GENERATION

BRUCE BERG OWNS the Record Stop, a popular new and used record store on King Street in Charleston, South Carolina. And while he sells albums and 45s from all eras and in all genres he says it's the music from the 1980s that keeps bringing back so many loyal customers.

Berg opened his first Record Stop in Ronkonkoma, Long Island, in 1974 ("I was at Woodstock," the seventy-seven year-old is quick to tell me) and soon found himself importing hard-to-find 45s from England for his punk-hungry clientele. "There was the Police, the Jam, all the British bands," Berg says. "They didn't have contracts here. We used to import the 45s and eventually the albums, and every Thursday night when the shipments came in it was like a party. We were a club house. I really had no competition for a few years. The only other ones were in New York City, in the Village . . . there was Bleecker Bob's and Golden Disc. They're all gone now. People would drive for an hour to go to my store and pick up their Stiff 45s and Chiswick label 45s." (Stiff Records was the label of Nick Lowe, Ian Dury, Wreckless Eric and Elvis Costello, and Chiswick's roster included the Damned and Sniff 'n' the Tears.)

These days, Berg tells me, "the most excitement in my store is when people find the Cure, Depeche Mode or the Clash" in the bins. (Henry Rollins of Black Flag fame recently popped into the Record Stop and found his joy in a stack of classical music albums.)

"These people are living their youth," Berg adds. "That's what it is. Music is just a mirror of our good memories."

SQUEEZE PLAY

OKAY THEN, BRUCE. So here's a good memory.

It's September 10, 1997, and Glenn Tilbrook is playing a solo show at the Met in Providence, Rhode Island, which I'm attending with my friend Bob (a.k.a. soon-to-be father of a baby-to-be named Dylan). Alone on stage in blue jeans, a white T-shirt, with an acoustic guitar and a bottle of beer, Glenn starts singing "From a Whisper to a Scream"—a duet he sang with Elvis Costello in 1982.

Strange choice, a duet for a solo show.

So when Glenn abruptly stops strumming and asks for a co-singer from the audience, every hand shoots up to volunteer. Somehow he picks me. I climb on stage and sing the Elvis part. *"Oh it's not eeeeeee-asy to resist temptation . . ."* I give it my all. And I don't suck! (This was, of course, before we all had a social media-connected high-resolution camera in our back pockets, so there is no evidence to back this up. But I swear it's true.) The song ends, and I step offstage like a startstruck teenage zombie to accept high-fives from friends and strangers alike.

Later that night at the merch table, after a second encore, Glenn is greeting fans.

He signs my ticket "Thanks, Elvis."

I have never, ever, been the same.

Whenever I think of that experience I'm happily thirty-one years old again—which seemed old at the time but not so much now. I'll be twice that age soon enough.

About eighteen years later, on a Thursday night in 2015, my friend Bob and I are out on the town to see Glenn Tilbrook singing solo yet again, this time at the Brighton Music Hall in Boston. Leaning against the bar and watching the opening act wrestle with his acoustic guitar, I turn to tell Bob how cool it would be if I got called back up to the stage to sing with Glenn again tonight. But Bob's not standing right next to me. Glenn Tilbrook is. He's also watching the opening act, beer in hand.

"Um, um, Glenn," I manage to say. "Um, sorry, *Mr. Tilbrook*. I'm sorry to bother you, but years and years ago you pulled me up on stage and we sang a duet together."

Glenn smiles broadly, and for a delusional moment I think maybe he remembers me. "I don't remember that at all!" he says, feigning shock. (I learn later that this is often Glenn's "thing"—the duet with a random fan whenever he tours solo.)

Bob chimes in: "If you were his best friend, Glenn, he'd never let you forget it." The three of us toast our plastic beer cups. Close to fifty years old at that point, I nonetheless felt like a starstruck teenager yet again.

Glenn takes the stage. No second once-in-a-lifetime duet for me tonight. But I happily join the middle-aged crowd for a "Black Coffee in Bed" sing-along.

Almost as good.

It turns out that memories like this one bring more than just seconds of pleasure. One non-profit organization, Music & Memory, uses music to help people suffering from Alzheimer's tap into memories previously assumed erased.

"Music & Memory is built on the understanding that the music we love most is deeply embedded in our brains, shaping both our conscious thoughts and unconscious emotions," the organization's website explains. "This connection becomes even more powerful when someone is experiencing memory loss, dementia, or cognitive decline. Even when other parts of the brain struggle, music can serve as a key that unlocks memories and emotions. Familiar songs or beloved pieces tap into long-stored experiences, triggering recognition, connection, and engagement. By using music as an external stimulus, we can activate pathways in the brain, helping to stimulate cognition, spark awareness, and bring moments of clarity and joy— even for those who may otherwise seem unreachable."

Elvis Costello is a big supporter of Music & Memory; his biggest hit in the US was 1989's "Veronica," a song inspired by his own grandmother who was suffering from Alzheimer's.

So there's yet another good reason to keep listening, air-guitaring, and karaoking our songs. It's good for the soul *and* the brain. Keeping all those memories we're forgetting to remember to forget locked in our heads.

IT'S ALL IN MY MIND
(SO DON'T BE UNKIND)

MY CONVERSATIONS WITH WKKL's Bruce the Bear and the other Bruce from the record store and the B-52's fans in Vegas convince me that there's nothing weird about being in our fifties (or older) and still faithfully listening to the music we loved thirty-five, forty years ago. Maybe we had hair like Robert Smith when we were twenty, and maybe today we have hair like Peter Garret from Midnight Oil (e.g. "super bald.") But that's okay. Keep dancing in the kitchen. Just watch your step.

You may recall that at the start of this book I urged you "not to do the math" when you hear a favorite song from our new wave yesteryear. Instead, I urged you to "focus on the feelings." So let's do just that. Let's find out if our music makes us happy when we're feeling sad, or if the songs (and the persistent memories they carry) make us sad when we're happy.

Can both things be true at the same time?

Dr. Irene Merring is an LA-based psychotherapist (and a musician and singer) who in 2023 earned her Doctorate in Clinical Psychology with her dissertation "Punk Rock as a Component to the Humanistic Approach to Psychotherapy." Of course I have to speak with her. A punk rock therapist? Yes, please!

"A lot of my work is about radical self-acceptance," Dr. Merring tells me when we connect for a cross-country Zoom call. "We're not here to fix you. We're not here to make you a different person. We're here to make you the most authentic version of yourself." Punk rock songs and music videos are just some of the tools she uses to help her patients find and express their pent-up feelings.

On her website, Dr. Merring (who has a tattoo on her right arm with a lyric from the song "Homesick," a track on the Cure's indispensable 1989 album *Disintegration*: "And my eyes are bursting hearts in a blood-stained sky") explains her approach:

"So many of us struggle to find our place in this world and to live in our truth. We want to be seen, but we fear rejection. We want to use our voice, but we are afraid of judgment. If you are feeling this way, I can help. I bring a creative, punk rock, radical sense of self-acceptance to treatment. I believe in giving a voice to those who have been marginalized and do my best to advocate for the populations I am passionate about. I enjoy working with musicians and creatives, LGBTQ+, BIPOC, and BIPOC LGBTQ+."

Dr. Merring encourages her patients to share songs and music videos that speak to them, and she finds this approach a very effective conversation starter during therapy sessions. "I think punk has been really helpful with clients who don't always have the language to speak what's happening with them," she tells me.

Marginalized, disenfranchised and alienated youngsters from every generation have always coalesced around a specific niche genre of music to find their people and their voices. Hippies in the 1960s had psychedelic rock and started following around the Grateful Dead for the rest of their lives. Disco was the celebratory musical language of the gay community in the '70s well before the Bee Gees made it mainstream. Punks, new wavers and goths rebelled against the Ronald Reagan/Margaret Thatcher/yuppie mindset in the 1980s with our trench coats and our Sony Walkmans playing Joy Division. Gangsta rap gave voice to a generation dealing with systematic racism, police brutality and inner-city violence. Generation after generation, music is a shelter from the storm of daily life.

"My youngest client just turned fifteen, and my oldest client is sixty-seven," Dr. Merring tells me. "I think music in general is really helpful in trauma work. It helps to ground the person, especially if they have issues maybe with dissociating. Music will kind of bring them back into their body. In a lot of ways I think something like punk is really good with that because it is multifunctional. Punk is emotional and it's cathartic in a lot of ways—but there's also a sense of belonging and being seen in it as well. Music is a great way to get in touch with what's happening on the subconscious level."

Or, as Thomas Dolby sang in 1982, it's "SCIENCE!"

Mike Peters in concert in Boston, 2019.

IF YOU HAVEN'T SEEN THE 2016 musical/romance/coming of age film *Sing Street*, please do. It's a delightful little Irish film set in the mid-1980s about a fifteen-year-old schoolboy who finds love (and his true self) by forming a scrappy little new wave band with his goofy classmates.

In the movie, our hero Conor (played by Ferdia Walsh-Peelo) has all the usual reasons to fall under the spell of bands like the Cure: his family life is a bit unstable, his Catholic school teachers derive great joy from terrorizing their students, and he's trying to impress a slightly-older girl who seems so very worldly and sophisticated.

A mild-mannered Dublin lad when the movie begins, Conor is educated in new wave and post-punk playlists by his worldly and always-stoned older brother, and for Conor the music is liberation. He's soon dressing like a backup singer for Duran Duran and sporting a homemade version of the Cure's Robert Smith's towering haircut—much to the abusive disdain of the school's headmaster.

There's a lovely scene in the film when Conor's sixteen-year-old crush Raphina (played by Lucy Boynton of *Bohemian Rhapsody* fame), thanks her suitor for writing a song for her.

Raphina: "I really liked your song. It made me cry."

Conor: "Oh, I'm really sorry."

Raphina: "No, that's a good thing!"

They talk some more.

Raphina: "Will you write me a happy song sometime? I need a laugh."

Conor: "But what if I don't feel happy?"

Raphina: "Your problem is that you're not happy being sad. But that's what love is! Happy-sad."

These days, I often get a case of the happy-sads when I see or hear certain artists that first made an impression on me decades ago. And it's not just the *old* songs. The Cure's 2024 album *Songs From A Lost World* is a brutal and poignant rumination on aging, regret and death that brought many listeners, myself included, to tears. (It's catchy, too!) Another happy-sad example: seeing Crowded House play in Boston as they closed out their 2023 world tour—thirty-one years after dancing to "Better Be Home Soon" with Mom at my wedding and knowing that the band's co-founder and percussionist Paul Hester took his own life in 2005. Today, frontman Neil Finn's two grown sons play in the band. Depeche Mode's 2023 *Momento Mori*, released after the 2022 death of founding keyboardist Andy Fletcher, is a hauntingly beautiful and mature record.

Time flies, and happy-sad persists.

Dad died in his sleep on December 2, 2004, alone in a Florida motel room, his heart breaking one last time. He was seventy-two. He'd been on his way to meet Mom, who had flown down to Florida a few days before him; I think they were planning to relocate there permanently, like Jerry Seinfeld's TV parents. Instead of flying with Mom, Dad drove so he could visit some old friends and bank colleagues who live along the East Coast. I sometimes wonder if he slept in any of the same cheap motels I had when I'd driven alone to Florida with my *Those Songs* cassette tapes 14 years earlier. I also wonder now and then what he listened to on his car CD player on his long and solitary ride down there. The Irish Rovers, perhaps? "The Unicorn?" Another song for the happy-sad playlist of life.

In 2016, Theresa was diagnosed with lymphoma, quite out of the blue. After more than twenty years treating cancer patients she suddenly found herself on the other end of the radiation beam and chemotherapy drip. Theresa had long been a big fan of the Alarm, seeing them in concert more than a few times with her best friends from Dorchester between the carefree 1980s and her 2016 diagnosis. (Theresa's friends were named Mary Theresa and Mary, of course. Nice Irish Catholic girls.) As an '80s music fan, you likely know that Mike Peters, the Alarm's frontman, songwriter and soul, fought lymphoma and other cancers five times between 1995 and 2025, eventually founding the Love, Hope, Strength Foundation to encourage voluntary bone marrow testing. "Strength" (1985) is one of the Alarm's most powerful songs, with lyrics written ten years before Peters' initial diagnosis but frighteningly prescient:

Give me love
Give me hope
Give me strength
Give me someone to live for
Who will light the fire
That I need to survive?
Who will be the life blood
Coursing through my veins?

The lyrics echo the hymn we sang at Amy's funeral:

Strength for today
And bright hope for tomorrow.

Theresa did well with her cancer treatments, briefly sporting a Sinéad O'Connor haircut and pulling it off with grace, and she later volunteered for the Love Hope Strength Foundation, working a table at the entrance to all sorts of concerts in Boston in an effort to sign up volunteers for bone marrow matching tests. Since its creation in 2006, the Foundation has registered more than 250,000 people onto blood stem cell registries, and more than 4,500 of those have been identified as potentially life-saving matches.

On July 19, 2017—just a year after her diagnosis—Theresa and I went to see Mike Peters play at a small oceanfront nightclub on Cape Cod called the Beachcomber. We saw him again on August 21, 2019 at Boston's Paradise Club. Both shows were electric. Despite his ongoing battle with blood cancer, the man was a relentlessly positive and generous performer.

Theresa, Mike Peters, Mary Theresa, and Mary.

Mike Peters died on April 29, 2025, at the age of sixty-six. Many of his songs—"Unsafe Building," "Rain In The Summertime"—remain some of the most bittersweet Theresa and I know, and when they come on the radio we both shake our heads and quietly sing along, at once both celebrating and mourning this inspirational Welshman. (If you haven't seen the 2017 Mike Peters documentary *Man in the Camo Jacket*, please do. Talk about happy-sad!)

"Happy-sad" is a powerful combination. The Smiths recorded some of the saddest dance songs of the 1980s; just try to sit still during "Barbarism Begins at Home," the catchiest song you'll ever hear about child abuse. With upbeat melodies and downbeat lyrics, "Love Will Tear Us Apart" by Joy Division, "Vicky Verky" by Squeeze and "Don't You Want Me" by the Human League are good examples of happy-sad music. "Dance away the heartache," Brian Ferry also reminded us in 1979. "Dance away the tears.")

I felt the need to dig more into the idea of happy-sad, as I suspected I'm not the only Gen Xer who feels this way sometimes. Or feels this way a lot. And so I jumped online and stumbled upon the work of Dr. Sandra Garrido, a Senior Research Fellow in Brain Sciences at the MARCS Institute for Brain Behavior and Development in Sydney, Australia.

Dr. Garrido's many books include *Why Are We Attracted to Sad Music?* and *Music, Nostalgia and Memory: Historical and Psychological Perspectives*. Now here's a person who *must* be able to help me (on behalf of my fellow Gen Xers) better understand why listening to our favorite '80s music involves our hearts as much as our ears.

In her research (which she is quick to remind me builds on the work of two earlier researchers, Paul Trapnell and Jennifer Campbell), Dr. Garrido explains there are five primary "mechanisms" that our ears and brains and hearts use to turn music into mood and emotion:

#1-Reflection: This happens when, prompted by a particular song, the listener reflects on life events and takes a few moments to reframe or reappraise those events. ("Gosh, this Duran Duran song really reminds me of that girl who broke my heart in 1984—but come to think of it now, I *was* kind of an asshole that summer . . .")

#2-Catharsis: This occurs when we use a song as a vehicle to expel the emotions we're currently experiencing. ("I hate my job so much that I sat in my car in the employee parking lot at lunch and cranked 'Shout' by Tears for Fears over and over again for forty minutes. I hope no one saw me shouting at the steering wheel!")

#3-Solace/connection: This emotional state emerges when a certain piece of music helps the listener feel part of a community and that they are "seen." ("The kids in drama club are so much cooler than everyone else in school. They love Joy Division too—just like me!")

#4-Rumination: This one is important for aging Gen Xers. Ever wake up one day and realize you've only been listening to the Cure's 1989 album *Disintegration* on repeat for the last three months—while obsessively doom-scrolling the headlines on your phone and thinking how things were so much simpler forty years ago? "Music can be used as a form of rumination resulting in a worsening of mood, even if it initially triggers memories that cause a happy emotional response in the short term," Dr. Garrido explains in her research.

#5-Aesthetic pleasure: This one is self-explanatory. Sometimes we seek out certain types of music simply because we think it's beautiful. Simple as that. We hear a particularly well-crafted song from our formative years like R.E.M.'s "Cuyahoga," the Style Council's "Shout to the Top!," or Elvis Costello's "Jack of All Parades" and all we can do is smile and shake our heads in wonder at the sheer artistry on display.

Dr. Garrido's "five mechanisms" gets me thinking: Back in high school or college, when we first listened to new wave and punk music, the emotional math was most often 2 + 3 = 5. Meaning—in our emotionally-loaded and sonically complex alternative music, we found an outlet ("catharsis," #2) for our ill-defined anger, fear and anxiety and we gained a sense of community ("solace/connection," #3) when we discovered other freaks and geeks who liked our songs and our bands, too. So, 2 + 3 = 5, the "5" being mechanism #5, which is the "aesthetic pleasure" we couldn't derive from Journey, White Snake or Guns N' Roses.

Today, as Gen X frets about retirement, the environment, our kids, our elderly parents and those strange-looking moles on our forearms, I realize the emotional math more often goes like this: 1 + 4 = 5. Meaning: "reflection" (#1) mixed with "rumination" (#4) drives us to listen to our old favorites—and ultimately yields #5, "aesthetic pleasure."

Which is a complicated way of saying music has the power to make us "happy-sad."

I ask Dr. Garrido to explain why it's important to be mindful of the headspace we're occupying when we turn to music for medicinal use.

"The distinction between rumination and reflectiveness is pretty important," she tells me via our email exchange. "You can read some work by Trapnell and Campbell on that, since this was a distinction they came up with. Reflectiveness is a healthy process of thinking about one's own experiences and feelings and working through them in a positive way, while rumination tends to involve getting stuck in a negative perspective. Reflection helps people to work through things and come out the other side feeling better, while rumination is by definition about going over and over the same negative thoughts without getting anywhere. It is more emotion-focused than problem-solving-oriented and hence is a less helpful coping style."

I tell her a little about how my brother JB and his music cast a long shadow over this book, and over my life in general.

"What you're talking about is really nostalgic rumination, I guess," she tells me. "I have written about that a bit. It too can be helpful or unhelpful. If listening to this music on repeat is making you feel connected, energized, happy, then that's great! If it is making you feel worse about the present then it's not such a helpful habit."

OUR MIXTAPES,
OURSELVES

MIXTAPES AND PEOPLE HAVE a lot in common. Both can surprise you with their highs and lows, their poetry, their passion, and their depth. Both can tell stories that make you cry or make you dance with joy. Mixtapes, like people, can be emotionally manipulative, brutally honest, silly or sweet—sometimes all of these things within the course of the same 90 minutes. Exuberance, anxiety, anger and longing can live on the same cassette and in the same heart.

Mixtapes, like people, can rewind, going back—over and over again—to the stuff that brings happy-sad smiles and tears. But excessive rewinding can stretch a person, and a mixtape, dangerously thin.

Mixtapes and people can both fast-forward, trying their best to jump over the stuff they don't really enjoy. But that stuff is still there, in life and on the tape, and sometimes it's hard to time the jump just right—and you end up right back in the middle of the thing you were trying to avoid.

Mixtapes, like people, get old. They get worn out. And they die. Some sooner than others. As Crowded House sang in 1991, "It's only natural."

Mixtapes, however, are much better at pausing than people are. Sometimes it's not so easy to simply take a deep breath and reflect on where you've been, where you are, and where you're headed. But there comes a point when you have to do just that.

Elvis Costello told me this would eventually happen, when, in 1989 on his album *Spike*, he sang a song called "Deep Dark Truthful Mirror." Go listen to it, if you can. It will challenge you to face up to painful truths that someone might love you too much to say.

The reflection in *my* deep dark truthful mirror has been telling me for a while now that it's time to adjust the knobs on my emotional equalizer.

UNHEARD WORDS
AND UNHEARD MUSIC

NONE OF MY FAMILY EVER really "got over" JB's death, and why would they? We all keep a part of him alive in our own particular ways—quietly, privately, or in a slightly disproportionate manner, like me. His initials or his birthday are part of an online password or two, I'm sure. He's a picture in a frame on a crowded bookshelf, an unexpected smile that surfaces when a certain song comes on the car radio.

I have to give Mom a shout-out here for how she dealt with the loss of her first-born son. A year after JB left us—a year filled with wrenching grief—Mom somehow found the strength to hit the speaking circuit, talking with wide-eyed youth groups about AIDS, about my brother's life and needlessly early death.

By choice I never saw her give one of her talks. But I heard, consistently, that her presentations were riveting, non-judgmental, and actionable. The kids in the audience left Mom's talks knowing two things with certainty: that parents truly, madly, deeply love their children, and that every sex-and-drugs-and-rock-and-roll-related decision they'll make will have real consequences, someday. Lessons learned, attitudes adjusted, the world was a slightly safer place for these kids after having heard Mom tell JB's story in the context of a global epidemic. Not nearly enough people were talking to young adults this meaningfully and directly in the early 1990s.

How Mom found the energy to do this for more than a year at dozens of speaking events is beyond me; it pains me just writing about this three decades later. But in her well-attended talks with young people at Catholic churches throughout New England, Mom momentarily brought JB back to life—and doubtlessly saved a few lives in the process.

Here's an excerpt from a thank you note from a local school's student council president, circa 1994: *Just knowing that people care enough to spend a day at our school has made students understand how very real AIDS is . . . you are doing so much good by speaking about your son's tragedy. It must be very difficult but you are making a difference . . .*

For JB, that's a legacy way cooler than any eclectic record collection.

So. Fast-forward to June 19, 2025—thirty-three years since JB died—and with my fifty-ninth birthday fast approaching I decide

I'm going to give myself the gift of closure: it's time to make my big brother a new mixtape and deliver it to his grave and maybe get on with my (musical/emotional) life. It's a horrible thing to quantify, but I can't help myself: JB has been gone longer than he was here. I have no intention of forgetting about him—"Don't You (Forget About Me)!"—but perhaps it's time to reframe how and why I listen to those songs—our songs. A little less rumination, a little more action, perhaps?

The cemetery is about sixty-five traffic-filled miles north of where I live today—perfect for a 90-minute mixtape to play in the car for the journey. It's been at least twenty-five years since I paid my respects in person, and the last time I visited I emptied a box of Honeycomb cereal, one of his favorite snacks, onto the ground beneath his headstone. This time I'll leave behind a mixtape of eighteen songs he never got a chance to hear but that I know he would have loved had AZT come to the market just a little sooner.

Making this mixtape was really, really difficult, but not for the reason you might expect. Of course it hurt, emotionally, trying to narrow down three decades of tragically unheard music into a 90-minute mix. Like, it hurt a lot. But the real challenge was in just making the damn thing itself.

Back in the day, it was easy enough to record an LP or a 45 or even a track from a CD onto a cassette recorder that was connected to the analog stereo stack. With a dual cassette deck you could even transfer a song from one cassette tape to another. All you needed was a small tangle of red and white RCA cables and a quick index finger to hit "pause" on time.

Today? Half the songs I want JB to hear, wherever he may be these days, are MP3 files living on old laptops, or in the cloud on my Amazon Music account, or out there in Spotify/Pandora/Apple Music-land. In the 1980s I knew very well how to get music from point A (an album) and B (the B-side of a 45) to point C (a blank cassette). Now, music flows to and from points A through Z, colliding with a whole bunch of digital 1s and 0s in the way.

It took me almost two weeks and a couple of low-fi workarounds, but I managed to finish the tape. I named it *Unheard Music*, and adorned it with a picture of us taken sometime in the mid-1980s.

The tape.

Listening to the tape on the drive to the cemetery was also difficult, but again more for technical reasons than emotional ones. Detroit and Japan stopped putting cassette players in cars in 2010, so to listen to the tape I had to connect my no-name cassette-to-MP3 device to a portable Bluetooth speaker via AUX cable. And then I had to charge that speaker via a USB cord before I left the house. And I had to make sure the cassette player had fresh AA batteries. The contraption looked like a mini nuclear warhead cobbled together by new wave terrorists. My kingdom for a proper analog boombox bouncing around the backseat like Gus and Bob and I shared back in Stoughton.

Here's the playlist, a collection of songs loaded with obscure and obvious lyrical references to love, aging, loss and death.

Side 1

"All I Ever Am," The Cure (2024)
"Nails in My Feet," Crowded House (1993)
"Ode to My Family," The Cranberries (1994)
"Everybody Out There," Paul McCartney (2013)
"Feed the Tree," Belly (1993)
"Boots of Spanish Leather," Nancy Griffith (1993)
"Miracle Drug," U2 (2004)
"London's Brilliant Parade," Elvis Costello (1994). I added this because it's a terrific song that celebrates a carefree afternoon exploring London—and because it makes me think of my brother JB's first and only visit to London a few months before he died. Mom and Dad took him there. Getting around in a rented wheelchair, JB somehow found the time and energy to buy me a book about the Cure. He wrote me a note on the inside cover:

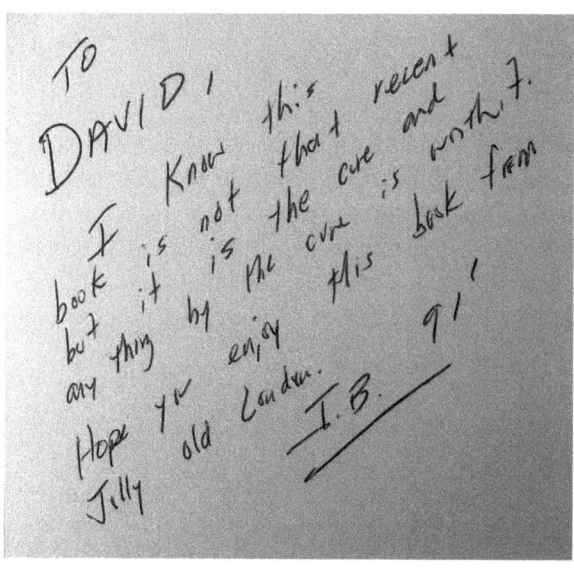

To DAVID!
I know this recent book is not that is the cure and worth it. but it is by the cure book from any thing by enjoy this
Hope yr old London. 91
Jelly
I.B.

Side 2

"I Can Never Say Goodbye," The Cure (2024): (The lyrics, about a dark and malevolent force coming to take the life of the singer's brother, are just too spot on.)
"I Put a Spell on You," Bryan Ferry (1993)
"Jacqueline," Franz Ferdinand (2004)
"Hold On To Yourself," Nick Cave and the Bad Seeds (2008)
"Where's My Everything?," Nick Lowe (1994) (A super-clever song about aging, regret and rumination.)
"Natalie," Bell X1 (2005)
"Rush Across the Road," Joe Jackson (2008)
"A Sigh," Crowded House (2007).

Of course, I included two additional songs on JB's new tape—the A-sides of the two 45s Amy gifted me before she passed back in 2023, by the Buzzocks and the Cure. JB already knew those songs and had probably played his drums to them hundreds of times, but it seemed appropriate to squeeze these two tracks in at the end of Side 2. I honestly can't remember if Amy and JB ever met, but I know they would have liked each other.

I pressed play as I backed my car out of my driveway in the early morning dark, and I carefully flipped the tape to Side 2 after driving forty-five miles or so, the sun rising in my rearview mirror.

I've always been a shameless car singer, but I didn't sing along this time. I just listened.

The tape ended about five minutes before I arrived at my final destination.

CEMETERY GATES

HOLY CROSS CEMETERY & Mausoleum spans 180 acres and is home to over a half-million dearly departed, but for some delusional romantic reason I was sure that, after a quarter century away, I'd magically find my way back to where JB is buried with ease. I walked up and down rows and rows of stone markers thinking "that tree looks familiar," or "this feels like where it happened" more than a few times, to no avail.

After close to forty minutes of scanning names—all those people, all those lives, where are they now?—I gave up and went back to my parked car.

On the passenger seat, tucked beneath my nuclear-powered portable tape deck thingy, was a map of the cemetery I'd printed out the day before, from its website. I had also called the administrative office to ask for the precise location of the grave, "just in case" I couldn't find it on my own. The coordinates were scrawled on the paper with a black magic marker.

I hated that I needed a cheat code to find the spot.

JB, my favorite amateur drummer, is buried with Mom's mom, our nana, who was a talented and energetic ragtime piano player. I like to imagine the two of them are jamming together out there somewhere right now. At last I found my place. Nana's full name and dates, 1907–1984, and JB's, 1960–1992, are etched onto either side of a single stone marker, like the labels on two sides of the same mixtape.

I used the plastic mini library card attached to my car keys to scrape off the pale green lichen that had bloomed around and over the letters of their names.

When I was done, I just stood there and stared into the sun with my eyes closed for a couple of minutes.

Then I placed the tape on top of the stone and left.

I had briefly considered making a duplicate of JB's new mixtape so I could listen to it again on my ride home, but for some reason it didn't feel right and I opted against doing so. Let my brother be the exclusive caretaker of this heartfelt stereogram, I figured.

Instead, I drove the 90 minutes back home music-free, actually enjoying the silence. At last.

EPILOGUE

MY KIDS INTRODUCED me to a fair amount of modern alternative music in the 2000s, and I actually like a lot of it. Orla Gartland. American Football. Soccer Mommy. Twenty One Pilots. the Black Keys . . . and I've never heard a weak track from the Hives or Franz Ferdinand, so it's not like I block my ears whenever a song comes on that was recorded after 1989. Still, I experience a ridiculous amount of joy when I catch one of my kids singing along to a classic '80s new wave tune. Whenever I express surprise that they know all the lyrics to those songs, the answer is always the same: "I grew up in your house, Dad."

Evan, my oldest, plays a mean electric guitar and sometimes fiddles around with the banjo, the piano and even an old drum kit.

Julia, our middle child and a Beatles fan from the start, was just six years old in 2004 when she insisted we name our new dog Ringo. At her wedding last year, our father-daughter dance was "In My Life." Her idea.

And Ethan, my youngest, recently told me that he really needs to listen to more R.E.M.

I done good, I suppose. Theresa, too. Perhaps we'll turn out like our songs, those songs: remembered many years from now with love, a small smile, and a little pogo dance in the kitchen.

May you be remembered this way, as well.

P.S. Mom recently turned ninety-one and has become close friends with a local radio DJ, who gives her a cheerful shout-out every weekday morning on his easy-listening show. More than seventy years after her high school yearbook entry revealed her "heart's desire" to be on the radio, her dream has finally come true.

BONUS TRACKS: THOSE SONGS

Part 3

"Sweet Thing," The Waterboys

"Hounds of Love," Kate Bush

"Take a Chance With Me," Roxy Music

"That Voice Again," Peter Gabriel

"Sinking," The Cure

"(Forever) Live and Die," O.M.D.

"Ceremony," New Order

"Coming Up Close," 'Til Tuesday,

"Rubber Ring," The Smiths

"Riot Act," Elvis Costello

"World Leader Pretend," R.E.M.

Part 4

"Kingdom of Rain", The The and Sinéad O'Connor

"Be Still My Beating Heart," Sting

"Verdi Cries," 10,000 Maniacs

"Closedown," The Cure

"All Come True," World Party

"Suedehead," Morrissey

"What If We Give It Away?," R.E.M.

"Tomorrow's World," Joe Jackson

"Smoke Rings," Winter Hours

"Fall on Me", R.E.M.

Part 5

"Cities in Dust," Siouxsie and the Banshees

"All In My Mind," Love and Rockets

"London Calling," the Clash

"Catapult," R.E.M.

"A Little Murder", the Buck pets

"Ascension Two," Pete Townsend

"Lie Detector," Screaming Blue Messiahs

"Yeah Yeah Yeah Yeah Yeah," the Pogues

"Devil Inside," INXS

"I'd Pay the Price," Cruel Story of Youth

Part 6

"Birds Fly (Whisper to a Scream)," Icicle Works

"Mad World," Tears for Fears

"Rock Non Stop (All Night Long)," Big Audio Dynamite

"Other 99," Big Audio Dynamite

"Living Through Another Cuba," XTC

"Mediate," INXS

"Darkness," Human League

"Lost Weekend," Wall of Voodoo

"You Hit the Spot," Graham Parker

Part 9

"I Love a Man in a Uniform," Gang of Four

"If You Leave," O.M.D.

"A Girl in Trouble (Is a Temporary Thing)," Romeo Void

"Go!," Tones on Tail

"The Dead Heart," Midnight Oil

"It Must be Love," Madness

"Promised You a Miracle," Simple Minds.

Part 10

"Generals and Majors," XTC

"The Stand," The Alarm

"I Got You," Split Enz

"Age of Consent," New Order

"Panic," The Smiths

"Love Plus One," Haircut One Hundred

Part 11

"What's the Matter With You," Split Enz

"Bizarre Love Triangle," New Order

"I Must Not Think Bad Thoughts," X

"I Want You Back," Hoodoo Gurus

"You Got the Look I Like," Nick Lowe

"Jump in the River," Sinéad O'Connor

"Too Far Gone," The Feelies

"... This Town ...," Elvis Costello

"The New World," X

"You Belong to Me," Elvis Costello

"True Love Pt. #2," X

Part 12

"Sex & Drugs & Rock & Roll," Ian Dury and the Blockheads

"(I Don't Want To Go To) Chelsea," Elvis Costello

"She's So Modern," The Boomtown Rats

"New Life," Zones

"Another Girl, Another Planet," The Only Ones

"Whole Wide World," Wreckless Eric

"Because the Night," The Patti Smith Group

"Beat My Guest," Adam & The Ants

"Fire in Cairo," The Cure

"Goodbye," The Psychedelic Furs

Part 13

"Space Oddity," David Bowie

"Slave to Love," Roxy Music

"Promises, Promises," Naked Eyes

"It's My Life," Talk Talk

"I Confess," The English Beat

"The Killing Moon," Echo & the Bunnymen

"Must I Paint You a Picture," Billy Bragg

Part 14

"Darkness," Human League

"Love Plus One," Haircut One Hundred

"Heaven (Must Be There)," Eurogilders

"Put Your Back To It," November Group

"Play for Today," The Cure

"Smalltown Boy," Bronski Beat

"October," U2

"Listen," Tears for Fears.

ACKNOWLEDGEMENTS

REMEMBER THAT MOVIE *Inception*? Great Hans Zimmer soundtrack. Anyway, in the movie, Leo DiCaprio and his clever, well-dressed friends surreptitiously implant ideas into the heads of unsuspecting victims. Doreen Iudica Vigue did that to me in 2016 when she read my first music-related blog post and told me "this needs to be a book." Thanks for the inception, Doreen.

I greatly appreciate the very honest and direct feedback I got from a few folks who were kind enough to invest precious personal time in reading early drafts: Gabriela Allen, Greg Wagner, Patricia Linsley and many more. Thanks for making me make this book better.

Thank you, Mr. Stanz, for being the musical and cinematic wizard behind the curtain for a very, very long time. You made a lasting impression.

And to Mom, Dad and my sibs, who each have their own version of this story.

A special thanks to Brian Eno for his 1979 album *Ambient 1: Music for Airports*, which has been my go-to background music for writing since 1986. It's truly "as ignorable as it is interesting," making it perfect for writing with tinnitus. (Oh, and thanks, Bob Mould, for giving me tinnitus in 2004 at your show at the Paradise Club in Boston! You're never too young for ear plugs, my friends!)

I'm grateful to my wife, my kids, and rescue doggos Duncan and Luna for putting up with my incessant four-fingered typing, and with me in general.

Gus and Bob: thanks for being a consistently strong and clear signal in a world filled with static, especially these days, forty-five years later.

Tip o' the red pencil to Bill Berry, Jim Ayres, Deb Geisler and Edward Wall for their Sisyphean efforts to teach me about spelling and punctuation. Gio Barone, please keep writing: you're very good at it.

And a big fist-bump for Maia Betts, LICSW—the world's greatest therapist, who, when I told her I was writing a book about new wave music, surprised me by asking: "Like Kraftwerk?"

Everyone's a music fan.

www.ingramcontent.com/pod-product-compliance
Lightning Source LLC
Chambersburg PA
CBHW051652120626
46551CB00015B/2327